PRAISE FOR
SEARCHING FOR ENOUGH

Searching for Enough quickened my heart for Jesus, refueled my calling as a pastor, and deepened my love for the people God has placed in my life to serve.

DAVID NASSER, author of *Jumping through Fires*

Tyler Staton discerningly identifies and illuminates the longings of the human soul. Through moving stories from his community, he deftly depicts a way forward. In a time of cynicism, confusion, and disbelief, this book is a force of buoyancy, clarity, and hope.

DR. DARREN WHITEHEAD, pastor of Church of the City, Nashville, and coauthor of *Holy Roar: 7 Words That Will Change the Way You Worship*

This book is annoyingly good. I picked it up for a quick skim before getting on with a packed to-do list. But try as I might, I could not read it quickly. *Searching for Enough* charms you into slowing down and drinking deeply. If you've got something urgent to do, perhaps picking up this book isn't the wisest idea. Otherwise, sit back and savor the beauty and life you will find within.

KATIA ADAMS, senior pastor of The Table Boston and author of *Equal*

T0053503

The days of childlike faith seem to have slipped beyond our culture moment. The best of us wrestle with the darkness of the world and God's work of redemption in the midst of it all. In *Searching for Enough*, Tyler Staton compellingly addresses both the angst and the hope we feel deeply in our souls and paints a captivating way forward with Jesus. This book is rich and accessible, and watching Tyler lead and embody what he writes gives it deep authenticity. I highly commend this book.

JON TYSON, lead pastor of Church of the City
New York and author of *Beautiful Resistance*

Tyler Staton has written a beautiful book that from the first chapter puts a finger right on the spot of our collective pain and longing. We want to feel at home in our own skin, at home with where we live, at home with what we do and who we do it with. This all seems simple enough, but most of us have experienced how very hard it really is. *Searching for Enough* is a compelling road map back home to God that doesn't cast aside our doubts or provide easy answers. I'm looking forward to recommending this book to a lot of folks.

DAVID LOMAS, pastor of Reality San Francisco
and author of *The Truest Thing about You*

Tyler Staton is one of the most exceptional leaders I know in the rising generation. Compelling, articulate, passionate, and deeply earthed in real relationships, *Searching for Enough* is a book of hard-won insight outworked in the streets of Brooklyn, New York. One day I suspect that many people in America and further afield will know the name and appreciate the teaching of Tyler Staton. The release of this, his first book, is a milestone, and I encourage you to join him on the journey. It's going to be a wild ride!

PETE GREIG, 24-7 Prayer International and
Emmaus Road Church, Guildford, UK

For those who hunger for more of God, who grow weary of shallow and cliché approaches to Christian spirituality, who seek direction and discernment in a world of doubt and false promises, Tyler Staton offers something richer, deeper, and ultimately more satisfying. *Searching for Enough* illuminates the solid path on which to follow the call of Jesus in our contested times.

MARK SAYERS, senior leader of Red Church, Melbourne, and author of *Strange Days* and *Reappearing Church*

For anyone who has the courage to admit they're struggling with the wound of not-enoughness and are ready to set out on a spiritual journey to search for more, here's my encouragement: get this book and let Tyler Staton be your guide. Trust me, you won't regret it!

PETE HUGHES, senior pastor of King's Cross Church (KXC), London, and author of *All Things New*

SEARCHING
FOR
ENOUGH

THE HIGH-WIRE WALK

BETWEEN

DOUBT AND FAITH

TYLER STATON

ZONDERVAN
BOOKS

ZONDERVAN BOOKS

Searching for Enough
Copyright © 2021 by Tyler Staton

Requests for information should be addressed to:
Zondervan, *3900 Sparks Dr. SE, Grand Rapids, Michigan 49546*

Zondervan titles may be purchased in bulk for educational, business, fundraising, or sales promotional use. For information, please email SpecialMarkets@Zondervan.com.

ISBN 978-0-310-36050-6 (softcover)

ISBN 978-0-310-36052-0 (audio)

ISBN 978-0-310-36051-3 (ebook)

Published in association with the literary agency of Wolgemuth & Associates.

Cover design: Tim Green | Faceout Studio
Cover illustrations: Private Collection© Robert Mann / Bridgeman Images;
    Callahan / Shutterstock
Interior design: Kait Lamphere

Printed in the United States of America

20 21 22 23 24 25 26 27 28 /LSC/ 15 14 13 12 11 10 9 8 7 6 5 4 3 2 1

AUTHOR'S NOTE

Personal names in this book have been changed. While all of the stories are real, I've changed people's names and other identifying details in order to protect the individuals' privacy. In one case, I compiled a number of conversations and stories into a single narrative.

To serve as a pastor in the life of even one of God's beloved children is a staggering privilege. It is my sincere hope and intention that this book honors the pastoral confidentiality assumed whenever anyone trusts me to walk a few paces of the spiritual journey by their side. Without the very real people who have sat across from me in coffee shops, wept with me in prayer, and served with me in mission, this work would be confined to the theoretical, but because of their stories, it is set in the grit and honesty of the everyday world.

To those who have grieved, questioned, celebrated, doubted, hoped, and lived the faith journey by my side—your stories are the real gift of this book. I am deeply grateful to each of you and hope I have honored and respected you in the pages that follow.

To Caleb Clardy—
you have given me far more as a friend
than I could ever repay,
so this book dedication will have to do.
Let's call it even.

CONTENTS

PART 3: *The Story of Our Twin*

FOREWORD

I wonder if the ache is a good thing.

You know the ache I'm referring to—not my ache or your ache, but *the* ache. Not the relentless, nagging desire for another raise or a new show to binge on Netflix or more ice cream or even a soulmate.

The *deeper ache*, the eternal ache under all the other ones—the stuff spirituality and religion and even the Western hedonism industrial complex is all built on.

The ache for "enough."

The desire across gender, race, class, and creed in all of us to feel: I'm *okay*. More than okay. Good. Happy. At peace. Safe. Full of hope for the future, but more than content in the reality of *now*. To feel what the ancient Hebrews called *shalom*—the inner experience of a soul at ease.

One way to frame the human story is, in Tyler Staton's language, as the search for enough. The search to feel—finally—at peace.

The driven careerist out to conquer the world and make it to the top, the artist willing to bleed her soul to "make it," the Tinder wanderer seducing his way through bar after bar, the travel junkie chasing one exotic passport stamp after another, the pastor preaching *another* sermon in the hope that her work for God will somehow quench her inner deficit of love from her family of origin, the scrappy high school student pulling all-nighters to make it into the Ivy League to get himself on the road to success.

These kinds of stories are the stuff of life, from kitchen-table gossip to the mythologies of every culture—ancient and modern.

Believer, nonbeliever; seeker, uninterested, or over it and disenfranchised. In-church, ex-church, and no-church. All of us are "searching for enough."

Even those of us who apprentice under Jesus and claim to have found our soul's ache—the one object that can actually satisfy our desire for eternity—even *we*, when we're honest, don't always feel the "enough" we are so quick to proclaim as our birthright.

Some rage at the gap between promise and felt reality; others pretend; most of us just keep quiet. But all of us *search* for more.

Tyler Staton has given us a beautiful book, one that is invigorating to the mind and a delight to read, yes, but make no mistake, it's a book for the *soul*.

As a writer myself, I'm a bit jealous: Tyler's first foray into writing is *much* better than my own. It's clear he's not just a pastor or even a communicator; he's an artist with a craft, each page an act of love and attention to detail. I pray that this book is the first of many I get to read from Tyler.

But as Tyler's friend, it comes as no surprise that his first book has depth and substance far beyond his years. I've long thought of Tyler as an "old soul" due to the wisdom latent in his inner life. Behind the pages you're about to read is a man of prayer, a man who is up early, day after day, to lift his soul to heaven in the quiet and begin each day with God. It shows in every paragraph.

Here's my encouragement as you begin to read. Take it slow. *Feel* your way through this book. It's full of great stories, killer quotes, and interesting asides—enjoy them. But let the Spirit of God do a slow, seeping work in your spirit. As you turn each page, open your heart just a little more to God.

You'll find far more than words waiting for you . . .

John Mark Comer

CHAPTER ONE

STUCK BETWEEN TWO UNSATISFYING STORIES

Good spiritual writing, among other things,
should help introduce us to ourselves.
Ronald Rolheiser

I was pedaling as fast as I could, narrowly passing between parked cars and bumper-to-bumper traffic on Manhattan Avenue. I clipped a side mirror with my backpack but pretended not to notice. There are unwritten rules in New York City, like if you're afraid of a scuff on your car, you live in the wrong place. Besides, I don't have time to stop. I'm ten minutes late. I'm always ten minutes late.

I don't have time for this meeting at all—not this week anyway. It's Holy Week, meaning the week that leads up to Easter, and I'm the pastor of a Christian church. We've got a service on Thursday night, a service on Good Friday, sunrise prayer, and a series of services on Easter Sunday. And this year, someone thought it would be a good idea to do a Holy Saturday service too. Whose idea was that? What combination of ignorance and foolishness made me agree to that?

Anyway, I don't really have time for a cup of coffee, but he was only gonna be in town for a few days. I'm cutting diagonally across an intersection while organizing thoughts for a sermon in my head (not recommended), hoping I'll still remember what I'm holding in my mind when we're done catching up.

"Look, I need to get this out in the open up front—I'm a couple beers in." That's how he started the pastoral counseling meeting he had scheduled with me. "I had a long lunch with a friend at the pub down the street, and, well, one thing led to another." I was meeting with Andrew, and I love this about Andrew. I'm being completely serious. I admire his honesty. He's one of the most forthright people I've ever met. The ten minutes he sat there waiting for me to arrive, predictably tardy, he must've nervously wondered if I'd smell the alcohol on his breath, if I'd judge him, or, even worse, "worry about him." *So*, he told himself, *I'll just get it out in the open.* And he did.

We were sitting outside, across a café table, in two ice-cold metal chairs. It was definitely not warm enough to sit outside. We both knew that, but neither one of us wanted to say it. We were the only ones who braved the sidewalk that afternoon, but this was early April, and after a long winter, the high 40s when the sun is out can feel tropical.

I hadn't gotten to see a lot of Andrew lately because he had booked a role on the cast of a major Broadway show that was on tour, which meant two things: his career was taking off and his home would be everywhere except his actual home for the next twelve months. He was back in Brooklyn for a week, a quick break from pretending to be someone else on a stage, to see a few old friends and catch up.

"A couple of beers in? No worries, man. You're on vacation. Besides, that'll probably only help you be just a bit more honest about whatever it is you want to talk about," I responded.

Normally, I'd open with some small talk before getting down to business, but as I already mentioned, this is Holy Week and I'm trying to pretend I'm not holding a few words in my head that felt inspiring when I clipped the side mirror of that salt-stained Camry.

We got to the heart of it right away. "When I moved to New York, somewhere in the back of my mind I was convinced that if I made it as an actor, I'd be somebody. When I say it out loud, I know I sound like the cautionary tale of an after-school special. I never consciously had that thought. I never said it to anyone, not even to myself. But somewhere, buried deep in my subconscious, I believed it.

"Then it happened. I was one of the lucky ones who broke into an impossibly exclusive industry more quickly than I ever thought I would, booking better roles than I ever thought I would, performing to larger crowds than I ever thought I would. My life right now is what I incessantly daydreamed about for as long as I can remember, and in spite of it all, I'm still the same person with the same problems and the same insecurities. I'm not any closer to being 'somebody,' whatever that means.

"So, what I'm getting at is this: it's not enough.

"My career will never be 'enough' for me. I always knew that in theory, but I really know that now."

THE "NOT ENOUGH" PROBLEM

I lost the sermon I was writing in the back of my mind. Andrew had me now—full attention. Because this is the story I hear constantly. The characters, setting, and circumstances change, but the central conflict is constant. I subconsciously bought the idea that life on my terms will deliver—that if I get what I want, I'll be happy, content, alive, at rest. But I'm not. I either haven't been able to arrange life on my terms, so it's not enough, or I've gotten life on my terms, and it didn't provide the internal fulfillment I thought came along with the external success. It's still not enough.

When our unspoken assumptions are proven false, it's like

someone pulls a block from the bottom of a Jenga tower. The shaky foundation we've been building on gets exposed for what it is, and the whole house falls.

Cara

"I'm finding life in Brooklyn hugely unsatisfying." I was sitting across another café table (this one indoors) from Cara, a woman in her early thirties from my church. Tears streamed down her cheeks as she began to recount her unique version of the same familiar story:

> I possess the ability to convince myself, again and again, that what I need in order to cope with reality is to regularly escape reality, so I'll spend this weekend bouncing between bars and clubs, drinking heavily, using drugs recreationally to enable more drinking, laughing and dancing, and for a moment, it works—I'm totally free. But peeling myself up from between the sheets of a stranger's bed the following morning, I face the horrible realization that this isn't freedom. It's something very different.

Drinks, then dinner, then more drinks, then dancing, then sex, then sober consciousness, then shame, then brunch, and finally the Sunday scaries—that weekly ritual of dreading another seven-day cycle through my ordinary life.

"My favorite indulgences aren't doing it for me. Escape doesn't work. It's not enough. The pursuit of pleasure as an end in itself somehow never ends in pleasure."

Cara's story is crystallized in Viktor Frankl's psychological discovery: "Pleasure is, and must remain, a side-effect or by-product, and is destroyed and spoiled to the degree to which it is made a goal in itself."[1]

The restlessness and anxiety that accompanies modern life

is not that simple though. We are not only pleasure seekers; we are also people of depth and substance.

Phil

It was around three o'clock on a crisp Tuesday afternoon in early autumn. I was sitting on the cheap, bonded leather sofa in my office. Across from me sat Phil, the vice president of a successful nonprofit, as he tried to breathe through a panic attack. His life was not driven by consumption. He had sacrificed much to be a part of the solution, pouring himself into a worthy cause. He was supposed to be satisfied and at peace.

"I'm giving up a bigger salary and many of the comforts that come with the corporate world for fulfilling work that sends me on my commute home each day knowing, 'What I do matters. I made a difference today.' That's supposed to be the exchange, right?"

That exchange wasn't working, not for him at least. He had come to the realization that it was time for a career change, and the thought that had him spiraling inward too fast for logic was this: *What am I gonna say the next time someone asks, "What do you do?" I've so identified with this cause and this role that I know it's time to let go, but I don't know who I am if I let go.*

The restlessness and anxiety that accompany modern life intensifies in a common realization: "It's not enough."

▪ ▪ ▪

We go by a variety of routes, but one way or another, we all end up there. This is one of those destinations we are insistent on visiting for ourselves. Cautionary tales like these seem helpless to prevent me (or you) from ending up in the same place at least once. We just can't take someone else's word for it. We've gotta find out for ourselves if there's an "enough" I can piece together under my own orchestration and control.

There's a difference between believing and knowing in the biblical imagination. We tend to think that a belief is deeper and more personal than knowledge. Belief involves a mixture of information and hope, but knowledge is just the recall of cold, hard facts—the answer to a math equation or the stats from a baseball game. In the ancient Hebrew understanding, it was the other way around. Beliefs are based on theory; knowledge is personal. The Hebrew term *yada* translates into English as "to know." However, it's a relational, experiential kind of knowledge, even used occasionally as a euphemism for sex. Knowing was thought of with that level of relational intimacy. Real, tangible experience is always implied in *yada*.

There are certain ideas we've bought into, and so we act in accordance with those ideas. Not everyone has touched a hot stove, but everyone believes it will hurt if you touch one. That's belief. Knowledge isn't theoretical; it's personal. Someone out there has put the palm of their hand on the glowing red coils of a hot stove. That's when belief got personal. That's knowledge.

I *believe* that another night out or a vocation with purpose or a curtain call with the cast in front of a standing ovation won't satisfy the deep longings of my soul and still the constant restlessness within. I've always believed that—in theory. But I *know* that now. Belief gets personal—it becomes knowing—when I'm standing at the counter ordering a large drip coffee with tears welling up behind my eyes because what made me feel wanted last night is exactly what's making me feel used this morning. I know it when I've lost myself if I can't identify by this position at a nonprofit, fighting this cause the next time I'm introducing myself to a stranger at a cocktail party. I know it when after the applause dies down, I'm back on the tour bus, wrestling with anxiety and the incessant itch of insecurity—*Weren't the cheering crowds supposed to relieve this?* Beliefs tend to live in the background of our lives. Knowing kicks the door down and confronts us.

Of course, there are less stark versions of this. These stories are the more extreme cases. Most of the time, it just looks like filling up life with a series of experiences we really, truly think will make us happy—coffee with a friend, a dinner reservation tomorrow night, plans after work, and an Airbnb in another city next weekend. We fill up our lives with many things, forever needing something good to look forward to, planning the next experience while having this one. We drink from the many wells we have dug for ourselves, convinced that if we keep drawing water, maybe this time it will quench our thirst. Henri Nouwen writes:

> Beneath our worrying lives, however, something else is going on. While our minds and hearts are filled with many things, and we wonder how we can live up to the expectations imposed on us by ourselves and others, we have a deep sense of unfulfillment. While busy with and worried about many things, we seldom feel truly satisfied, at peace, or at home. A gnawing sense of being unfulfilled underlies our filled lives . . .
>
> Boredom is a sentiment of disconnectedness . . . To be bored, therefore, does not mean that we have nothing to do, but that we question the value of the things we are so busy doing. The great paradox of our time is that many of us are busy and bored at the same time . . . In short, while our lives are full, we feel unfulfilled.[2]

BACK TO ANDREW

So I'm sitting there with my elbows on a cold, metal table in early April, listening to Andrew tell his version of our universal "not enough" story. But he didn't stop there. He kept going, and what he said next is the part of the diagnosis that tends to get left out.

"I don't know how to piece together the sort of life that will be 'enough' for me. I always *knew* that in theory, but I really *know* that now. But then I look at my conception of God, and honestly, that's not enough either."

He started to sound agitated now, not at anyone in particular, just angry at something he had thought long and hard about without seeing any way through.

"The biblical story of faith I was spoon-fed as a kid and have done my best to somehow hold on to as an adult is not enough for the complexity of the world I actually live in. IT'S NOT ENOUGH! I'M NOT ENOUGH, AND I'M NEVER GONNA BE. AND I KNOW I'M NOT SUPPOSED TO SAY THIS, BUT GOD'S NOT ENOUGH EITHER! AND I'M BEGINNING TO WONDER IF HE'S EVER GONNA BE."

And there it was. He said it. He said the thing that almost everyone I interact with about faith is circling around but doesn't have the words for. Spiritual breakthrough often starts with saying what you think and feel but are convinced you aren't "allowed" to say.

Andrew looked defeated, exhausted just from finally having said it. We both sat there without talking for a moment, the way you do when someone is so honest, when someone puts a mystery you've both felt at some time or another into words, and what's just been said isn't really something to agree or disagree with; it's something to feel the weight of, to be trapped together by the complexity of, to honor the honesty of.

STUCK BETWEEN TWO UNSATISFYING STORIES

Of course, it's not enough. The "story of the world" and the many forms of medication it offers to get us through our numbered days are not enough.

It's not enough to get everything I want. The fulfillment of my desires by my means only reveals a deeper longing beneath the symptoms I'm treating.

Hooking up with that guy won't make me feel desirable. Next weekend, I'll be right back where I started, and I'll want to reach for my phone again to swipe over to another random guy's apartment at the end of the night.

Getting that promotion won't make me feel content. I'll fight harder to keep it than I ever fought to get it, and the need to prove myself that I've conveniently rebranded as "drive" will just be revealed for what it is.

A week on a beach won't make my ordinary life feel more bearable. The circumstances of my life aren't what makes life unmanageable; it's my anxiety. I blame it on circumstances, but the truth is I've got something alive in my gut that's running full speed in every direction at once, and it will be just as alive on the return flight home when I'm dreading my ordinary life as it is on an average Sunday night when I can't even eat dinner because I'm so anxious about Monday morning.

So no, getting everything we want isn't enough. We can defer that realization for decades with distraction. Every time the honest realization "I chose this life by my own free will, and it's still not enough" gets close, we can just change the subject.

Maybe you want to put this book down, pull up Netflix, and stop thinking about this, but you also know that "changing the subject" isn't a life worth living. Distraction is fast food. It doesn't nourish us, but it does work for deferring hunger.

But what's the alternative? Jesus?

Are we seriously supposed to hope that the empty tomb of a first-century Jewish peasant somehow unwinds all this complexity?

The Christian church is hemorrhaging today's generation of young adults at a rate that's historically unparalleled because that story just seems too simple. It can feel insulting to get a simple solution to complex problems.

So here we are—stuck between two unsatisfying stories.

The story of the world leaves us wanting. It always has and always will, no matter how long we distract ourselves from that confrontation.

The story of Jesus is a compelling wonder, but if looking for life in an empty tomb is not enough for you, you should know you're not alone. You're in good company—even biblical company.

All four historically reliable biographies of Jesus' life culminate with a Sunday morning resurrection, and by late Sunday night, every living disciple has been wonderfully interrupted by the Messiah they had executed seventy-two hours prior—alive. Every disciple had a personal encounter with the presence of the living God on the original Easter Sunday—every disciple except Thomas.

THE TWIN

Thomas is my favorite. He's always been my favorite. I know Thomas. I am Thomas.

Thomas wasn't a fiercely rational cynic. To think of him that way would be to minimize a whole life down to one single moment, which is always a mistake. This is a man who left everything behind to follow a self-proclaimed Nazarene rabbi. He risked everything for Jesus. He witnessed miracles that left him rubbing his eyes in wonder, but he also faced rejection, confusion, and public disgrace for associating so closely with one who was called a criminal.

The very week of Jesus' crucifixion, Thomas steps forward in a critical moment to say he's ready to die with Jesus. He was ready to die with his rabbi, but he wasn't ready to live without him. And that's exactly what Jesus asked Thomas to do when he wouldn't say a word at his own defense hearing and took the death penalty like he was planning it all along.

Thomas isn't a cynic or even a skeptic. It's so much more personal than that. He's disappointed. He's hurt. Imagine pushing in all your chips, like he did on Jesus, and then the story ends in the kind of heartbreak so far outside of the realm of possibility that it blindsides you completely, leaving you in the kind of daze you never want to feel again. That's the Thomas we meet in his famous declaration of doubt.

He's hurting. He's confused. He's guarded. Life on his own terms wasn't enough; that's why he risked everything on Jesus in the first place, but how can he be the King of the everlasting kingdom from within a casket? Thomas isn't a doubter; he's a realist—calling it like he sees it.

"So the grave's empty, huh? Well, that's great, but I'm gonna need a lot more than that. If the rest of you are so desperate to believe, then go ahead, but I'm gonna piece together my actual life in the actual world. And if laughter, beer, and sex is as good as it gets . . . and if suffering is senseless and death is final and none of it amounts to anything more . . . then at least I had the courage to face it."

Thomas's resurrection reaction reads like God picked up a thirtysomething from San Francisco or Berlin or Melbourne or Brooklyn and sat them down in first-century Jerusalem on that defining Sunday morning.

I'm not sure I understand the experience of seeing someone alive on Sunday who was definitely dead on Friday, but I certainly understand the skepticism of hearing other people spread a holy rumor like that one and categorizing it as religious well-wishing at best. I see myself in Thomas. I see my friends in Thomas. I see my city in Thomas. Stuck between two unsatisfying stories.

> Now Thomas . . . was not with the disciples when Jesus came.
> So the other disciples told him, "We have seen the Lord!"
> But he said to them, "Unless I see the nail marks in his hands and put my finger where the nails were, and put my hand into his side, I will not believe."
>
> *John 20:24–25*

In essence, Thomas is saying, "If God wants me, he can come get me. I'm not hiding." Thomas was a realist—a strong-willed, fiercely logical realist—and that earned him a nickname: Doubting Thomas. That's a modern invention though.

His given name was Didymus, but everyone who really knew him called him by his Aramaic name—Thomas, which translates to "twin." The Twin—that's what all the other disciples called him, and it suits him . . . because, in a way, he's all of our twin.

Thomas is modern Western culture personified. A whole hemisphere is stuck between two unsatisfying stories. The citizens of the industrialized Western world enjoy more personal freedom, leisure time, career options, and entertaining distractions than anyone at any other time in human history, and yet the increase in personal autonomy and freedom hasn't led to increased happiness and fulfillment. Diagnosed and medicated mental illness has grown almost exactly parallel to these factors. The world's freest, wealthiest, most autonomous people are also the world's most anxious and depressed people.

Is there anyone you can identify with more in the Gospels than Thomas? Regardless of how you'd categorize your particular brand of belief or unbelief at this particular moment, plenty of us could say right along with Thomas, "It's not enough. The meaning I've tried to drum up for myself in this life is not enough to still my restlessness, but to be honest, I'm starting to think an empty tomb is not enough either."

MIRROR, MAP, MYSTERY

The book you're holding is a mirror, a map, and a mystery.

It's a *mirror* because Thomas is not a caricature. He is a real, honest, disillusioned, courageous seeker. The single moment of doubt he is often reduced to has a backstory with the same twists and turns as every human story. When we truly see Thomas, many of us will truly see ourselves. Some of us are disillusioned and disappointed with Christianity—sitting in Sunday pews bored out of our minds by the story we believe but don't know (a theory we believe objectively, not a life we know in a relational, experiential, subjective way). Some of us have walked away from the church—we are the real names and faces that are a part of the modern church's hemorrhage, whose most courageous spiritual moment may not have been admitting belief, but finally, reluctantly, bravely, admitting doubt. Finally, some of us are spiritually open seekers—those who are suspicious that there must be more than just the material world but who also have no context for Thomas, only anecdotal awareness of Jesus, and little to no interest in the biblical story. This book is a mirror for each of us because we are all starting with the same questions and looking for the same destination—what Jesus called "life . . . to the full."[3] Thomas our twin, a mirror. As you see him, I suspect you'll also see yourself.

This book is a *map* because Thomas's post-resurrection doubt is not an admonition to be avoided but an invitation to be followed. If we can see our condition in his, he can also offer us a way out. The life of the world's famous skeptic is more than just a diagnosis. Thomas can also be our guide. He offers both a picture of the stuck place we find ourselves in and a way to freedom.

This book is a *mystery* because Thomas's story doesn't end in philosophical enlightenment or rational answers; it ends in relational encounter. In the end, it is not an empty tomb that Thomas finds but an encounter with the living God. So what you're holding is not a guidebook full of answers (sorry to disappoint right at the beginning), but it is an invitation to encounter. If all we needed was the right information about God, he would have dropped an instruction manual down from the heavens. But he came as a person because the offer isn't information; it's life.

On the day that has divided human history more than any other, the day that started a movement so unparalleled that sociologists still marvel at an empire built on power undone by love, on that resurrection day, Thomas was stuck between two unsatisfying stories.

But to understand the way out, we have to first retrace the steps that got us here.

This book is divided into three parts, three stories:

1. The Story of the World
2. The Story of Jesus
3. The Story of Our Twin (Thomas)

THREE STORIES CAUGHT IN A SINGLE FRAME

© New York Post / Shutterstock

Early on a hot summer morning in the mid-1970s, Philippe Petit walked across a wire suspended between the iconic Twin Towers dotting the Lower Manhattan skyline. It was a spectacle.

Almost exactly twenty-seven years later, two commercial flights were hijacked and steered directly into those same Twin Towers, bringing them to the ground with thousands of casualties. It was also a spectacle—of the very worst kind.

A photo was snapped during Petit's jaunt across the wire that was meaningless for nearly three decades but then became iconic: a commercial plane caught behind the balancing man on the wire appears to be flying much too low, almost like it will hit the towers. Two moments that seem logically a lifetime apart are caught in a single frame. The stories overlap for just a moment.

That's what happened to Thomas. The story of the world and the story of Jesus seemed incompatible on resurrection morning. It was wishful thinking for any true realist. Then, for just a moment, the stories overlapped in a small upper room hideaway in central Jerusalem. Thomas, disenchanted by an empty tomb, encountered the presence of the living God.

That's the invitation for you. That's where this book is going. But to arrive at encounter, with all the context the Twin carried, we first have to understand the two unsatisfying stories we are stuck between. So that's where we'll begin.

Part 1

THE STORY OF
THE WORLD

CHAPTER TWO

UNFATHOMABLE POTENTIAL

Any fair explanation of the world and human history has to start with all of the very, very good we know in this life.

THE POTENTIAL OF THIS PLANET

Think for just a moment about the potential of the planet we all inhabit: Buried in the dirt beneath our feet are the bare ingredients of everything the world has been formed into. I'm writing these words from a coffee shop in Greenpoint, Brooklyn, and in the soil underneath me is the substance for everything I see—elements formed into this building that shelters me and controls the temperature, the materials molded into the transportation that got me here, the coffee beans I can smell being roasted, and the muffin I chose out of a clear bin of many tasty options—all of it, buried in the dirt beneath my feet.

This planet comes equipped with the bare materials that have become shelter, transportation, and nourishment to sustain life. That can be said of no other planet that has been discovered in recorded history.

But the potential of this planet is not limited to the bare essentials. Our world also contains beauty. It's not just that our world can sustain us; it's that it dazzles us. We have sounds like rain falling and birds chirping, but we also have the raw materials formed into instruments that channel sound into music, giving us Handel's *Messiah* and Miles Davis's *Kind of Blue* and Bob Dylan's "Hurricane." We have color, but it's not only the primaries. We find every imaginable shade that is rearranged in Michelangelo's painting of the Sistine Chapel ceiling and van Gogh's *The Starry Night* and Bushwick's graffiti murals. We have nourishment, but it's not just rations to keep us alive; it's herbs and spices and flavor that combine to make tikka masala and pad Thai and gumbo. Culture, in all of its variety and expression, with all of its flavors and sounds and movement, was born out of the once untapped potential of this planet. For a ball of dust floating around a star, that's pretty good.

Then there's society—the organization of people and customs into shared life. The resources buried under our feet have been gathered together to form towns and cities where people can communicate and cooperate and learn from one another. Human relationship is made possible and sustained by this planet. Amazing.

THE POTENTIAL OF A SINGLE HUMAN LIFE

Have you ever been in the room while a baby is born? I have. Twice. It's terrifying! The first time around, I got prepared with eight weeks of birthing classes, complete with breathing exercises and massage techniques. I watched Netflix documentaries that, to this day, I still can't un-see. At one point, I was packed into a tiny Manhattan apartment with about twenty other expecting couples, watching an old VHS tape of women giving birth in some kind of Amazonian tribal setting. Occasionally, I still wake up in a cold sweat with those images replaying in my unconscious mind. The point is, I got ready. I got as ready as any male can whose exposure to childbirth during the most formative years was limited to that one *Friends* episode when Rachel goes into labor and Joey has to take her to the hospital.

But nothing could have prepared me. Nothing could have prepared Kirsten (my wife) either. Nothing ever makes you ready. It's long and exhausting and terrifying and (seems to be) extraordinarily painful. And then, all of a sudden, it's the most beautiful celebration you can possibly imagine. You're laughing and crying at the same time, even though you promised yourself you're not that type of person. You can't explain the tears welling behind your eyes in any logical way. It's a mystery. A mysterious love comes alive in you that wasn't there before for a tiny person who has, so far, only suddenly forced an all-nighter on you and then made you hold them while covered in gross, filmy liquids.

And it's not just you. Every witness responds like this. I looked up for just a moment while holding Hank, my oldest son, in the first thirty seconds of his life, and one of the nurses had tears welling up behind her eyes. That's right. A labor and delivery nurse, who does only this, repeatedly, with strangers, five or six days a week, was moved to emotion by the potential of a new, unformed, uncorrupted, uninfluenced human life.

THE POTENTIAL OF A SINGLE MOMENT

Tommie Smith and John Carlos, two African American men, won gold and bronze medals, respectively, running the 200-meter race for the United States at the 1968 Summer Olympics—the same year Martin Luther King Jr. was assassinated, and the same year the Fair Housing Act was signed. The civil rights movement was very much alive and very much a part of the national conversation. As Smith and Carlos stood on the medal stand, facing their country's flag, "The Star-Spangled Banner" began to play, honoring the gold medal awarded to the United States. In that moment, Smith and Carlos each bowed their head and raised a black-gloved fist, the infamous "Black Power" salute associated with the leadership of Malcolm X. Tommie Smith called this gesture a "human rights salute," symbolizing the inherent worth of every human life.

In a single moment, without saying a word, a civil rights issue mostly confined regionally in one country became a global conversation.

© Universal History Archive / UIG / Shutterstock

In many ways, that was an ordinary moment. It was the same as the one that ticks by as you read this sentence. It was anticipated, felt, and then remembered like every other medal ceremony during the 1968 games. The world's best athletes descended on Mexico City with the dream of feeling the weight of a medal around their necks. They anticipated that moment, daydreaming about it to push through grueling training. Many of them got to experience it—to be washed in the anthem of their nation and showered in the applause of the crowd. They remembered it a thousand times over; they relished that moment.

But in the most important ways, this was an extraordinary moment.

This moment stands out from every other moment. Two men at these games who dreamed, not of the weight of a medal around their necks, but of the weight of a people on their shoulders. They didn't want to be washed in applause; they wanted to wash an entire race in dignity. And they got to experience what they anticipated, raising their fists with their heads bowed while fear, nervousness, hope, and, most of all, an unshakable resolve held them in that pose. Then the moment passed, but it lives on in memory—and not only in the memory of those two runners. This moment stands out just as profoundly, maybe even more personally, to those who did not run, to those for whom these fists were raised.

This is the moment for which the 1968 Olympics are remembered worldwide. It's the moment that defined the lives of these two men and helped redefine the lives of many they will never know. No one can truly understand the history of a race and a nation without also understanding this moment. The potential of a single moment in time is so much broader than just that single moment in time.

Another moment, 1989 Beijing. Students organized and led demonstrations promoting democratic thought in Tiananmen Square. The protests were eventually brought to an end on June 4 by a declaration of martial law that released armed military into Beijing to control the unrest by force, which they did. Civilian death totals are still inconclusive, but the basement is 180 and the ceiling exceeds 10,000.[1]

On the following day, June 5, a man who remains unidentified took a stand against the military force. He stood up against the Chinese military, which had been turned against their own country and were invading their own city. He walked out in front of a few tanks that were driving into the square and just stood, unwilling to move.

That moment was captured on tape by several national and global media outlets. The entire world took it in, not through the filtered commentary of an eloquent news anchor or a winsome journalist, but through the eyes of a witness. The world watched in horror through the perch of a cameraman as a man's life was threatened by his own government's use of weapons designed for war.

© Bettmann / Getty Images

Look closely at the photo. Look at the man's hands. He's holding his things—a shopping bag and maybe a backpack. We know almost nothing about this man, but his hands indicate that he was midway through an ordinary day. He was running errands or keeping appointments or going to class. We don't know the specifics, but it appears he was going about his ordinary life, carrying his things, and in a single moment of courage, he became—and remains—a symbol for defiance in the face of oppression.

Think of it—all the potential that exists within every single moment of every single life on this one orbiting, spinning ball each of us occupies space on right now. This world, this life, this very moment, holds within it unfathomable potential.

One More, November 9, 1989—the day the Berlin Wall came down. Twenty-eight years after Germany's largest city was forcefully cut in half, divided by ideologies that refused to cooperate, it was reunited. The entire world watched the historic spectacle, a public display of the triumph of hope and love.

The moment that moved the watching world to awe, though, came a few weeks later, on Christmas Day of that same year, when Leonard Bernstein composed a performance of "Ode to Joy" from Beethoven's Ninth Symphony. He altered the title to "Ode to Freedom" to mark the significance of the moment and assembled an orchestra from East and West Berlin, musicians who had been kept from sharing sheet music for nearly three decades. Together, these once divided people would usher the rest of us into the profundity of what we were all witnessing that Christmas night.

As the sound built and built to its exultant final movement, the hairs on the back of thousands of necks stood on end. Tears welled behind watching eyes—both of those breathing the cold December air in Germany and of those sitting in warm homes and staring speechless at a television screen all around the world. It was a spectacle. It was beauty that seemed to transcend this world. It was one of those moments that takes everyone beyond themselves—the breathtaking beauty of witnessing something that is "right," not because of an intellectual belief or even a decided conviction, but simply because it rings as pure truth in the deep recesses of every soul caught in its periphery.

A single moment that somehow emerged from the countless moments that led up to it and careened downward from it. What is that? How can one moment unite people that can't even hold a conversation through language, that may disagree ideologically, that may never share another thing truly in common? How can a bunch of very ordinary musicians—people who shivered at the cutting wind before picking up violin and bow, whose feet blistered on the long walk to the wall from their homes, who had arguments with their relatives just before picking up their instrument cases and heading out the door—how can they unite not just a divided city but a divided world with a well-played tune? That's the unfathomable potential of a single moment.

UNFATHOMABLE POTENTIAL

> *The Mighty One, God, the* LORD,
> *speaks and summons the earth,*
> *from the rising of the sun to where it sets.*
>
> **Psalm 50:1**

That's how the Psalms, the prayer book of the Bible, sum up the unfathomable potential woven into the fabric of this world.

There's some mysterious force out there, some creative designer with a weakness for beauty, or some unexplainable accident with phenomenal collateral damage (however you prefer to describe the source). No matter what you think of the truth claim of this ancient prayer, we all know the feeling that burned in the author when he wrote those words.

If you've ever seen the sun rise, you know the wonder that leads to this prayer. You've seen the painted sky fill with shades of blue, yellow, orange, and pink as light dances through the air and the clouds. You've seen an orange ball of fire move up along the sky as the world spins fast enough to dazzle you and slow enough to let you treasure the view.

Anyone who has ever taken a child to the zoo knows what's behind this prayer. You've watched them get wide-eyed with excitement, then terror, and then awe, all within the span of sixty seconds. You've witnessed someone taking in the variety of life on this planet for the first time. It's more than that small, uncalloused, innocent imagination knows how to handle.

Anyone who lives in a place with a winter—a real winter—knows what Asaph (the author of this prayer) knew when he wrote it. I'm not talking about the kind of winter that requires a jacket for a couple months. I'm talking about the kind you convince yourself is gonna be mild this year, every year—the kind that keeps snowing well into March, the kind of winter that leaves ash-colored ice clinging stubbornly to the sidewalk in mid-April. Anyone with a winter like that knows the feeling of the sun on their face on the first spring day when the temperature finally cracks 60 degrees. That spring day when everyone is somewhere, letting the sun hit their face and soaking it in.

Anyone lucky enough to know what "going home for the holidays" truly feels like has prayed this prayer in their own words. This prayer filled your being when, after a long, long drive, you sat up straight in the driver's seat for those last few miles.

That stretch of the drive that objectively looks like the hundreds of miles you've crossed emotionless, but what straightened you up isn't objective. These hills, these intersections, these bends in the landscape mean something different. These mounds of dirt aren't like the others. This patch of the earth isn't just another few miles to cross. This place is a monument to years gone by—memories you'll cherish forever and memories you'll try unsuccessfully to forget forever. No one escapes the nostalgia of their own adolescence.

This world is an amazing place. There's such unfathomable potential in the dirt we stand on and the air we breathe.

And a single life, an ordinary, uneventful life that won't be studied in a history book or memorialized in a hall of fame or documented in a police report—the most ordinary life is an extraordinary thing.

I remember being at the movies with my family when I was eleven years old. I thought the movie was boring and underwhelming. I looked over at my dad during the climactic scene. Tears were building heavily on his eyelids, waiting for that tipping point when gravity judges them too heavy to balance and so they begin to roll down his cheeks. I understand now what I didn't then—the ordinary days we get to live hold an endless depth. The more of these days you get, the more you realize what a gift this whole thing really is, and a movie about ordinary life becomes an extraordinary thing when you've got enough of your own ordinary life behind it to give it the proper weight. There's unfathomable potential—something heavier than can ever be weighed on paper by objective analysis—to every human life.

Then there's the potential of a moment—first report card, first time you score a goal, first recital, first kiss.

The moment you turn in that final paper, and you're done, just waiting on them to call your name as you begin your walk across the stage.

The penalty kick that went in, and your parents and a few others dotting the modest metal bleachers felt like the crowd at the World Cup.

The moment when the cheap DJ finally played a slow song at the school dance, and he actually asked you, chose you, and the song couldn't be slow enough.

The moment on your wedding night when everything is going by like a blur until it all slows down for just a second so you can take it all in—all the people you love the most in one place, celebrating the whole life you've got ahead of you with this other person. The moment fifty years later when you can feel the jewelry box in your pocket as you sit across from that same woman you've never grown tired of surprising—celebrating a half-century together at the early bird special at your favorite buffet. Life is filled with moments when the potential always poised behind them stands out, when the simplest, purest truth comes into focus: Life is good. It's really, really good.

Any objective analysis of this world and the life we have in it has to start there, but we know, of course that to stop there is to stop short of the full story.

CHAPTER THREE

RECURRING DARKNESS

God saw all that he had made,
and it was very good.

Genesis 1:31

The book of Genesis makes a pretty big deal out of Adam and Eve eating from the one forbidden tree at the center of the garden. But the intent was not to depict God as a harsh moral policeman. It's because the biblical story does not begin with a broken world in need of fixing. It begins with a perfect world—unformed, uncorrupted, uncontaminated, and wholly innocent—nothing but potential.

The first few chapters of Genesis are dismissed by most. Some grew up with this origin story, and familiarity has stripped away every last trace of power. Others weren't spoon-fed this story from a young age, so now as an educated adult with just the right combination of healthy skepticism and outright cynicism, talking snakes and magic fruit are a bit much. No matter which of these you identify with more closely, you're missing the real point of the story.

The opening of the Bible is written in the style of Hebrew poetry. The point of poetry isn't to argue about fact and allegory; it's to tell a story we recognize as true because it so pointedly reveals something true within each reader. It gives language to something we all feel but probably don't have the words for. That's what the opening chapters of Genesis are doing. It's a poem told just the right way so that when it ends, it lands on the chest of every hearer with such personal force that we are left motionless. Here's the larger point, the force of the poem: regardless of what we believe about the factual truth of the Genesis story, we all feel the truth of the Genesis story because it's a story that lives in us and retells itself in every last one of us. The Genesis story is every individual story.

God was at the center of every human life until that fruit was tasted. Since then, every human being has found their own unique way of putting himself or herself at the center of the story and demanding that the world cooperate. The biblical word for this is *sin*, but if you don't like that word, that's fine. It's a word that has been soiled for many by moralistic manipulation, outright legalism, or something much more personal. Sin isn't an explanation of moral boundaries, and it's a long, long way from legalism, so just throw the word out if it's problematic for you. I'm sure you've got your reasons. Substitute whatever term you prefer and keep going.

The terminology isn't that important. The concept the terminology represents—that's important. Essentially every great philosopher and thinker with a shaping influence on history agrees on the concept, even those who are oppositional on basically everything else. "Here, surprisingly, we find a great consensus. Freud and Plato, Karl Marx and Ralph Nader, Martin Luther King Jr. and Gandhi and Jesus all agree with this—something is terribly wrong with us and cries out to be put right."[1] G. K. Chesterton summarizes it like this: "Whatever else men have believed, they have all believed that there is something the matter with mankind."[2]

It's important to recognize that the concept the Bible calls "sin" is woven into the fabric of the world. To recognize this concept within yourself, though, is the critical part. Personal failure is a lot less about morals and a lot more about what occupies the center of your heart, because whoever or whatever holds that position is taking you somewhere.

SOCIAL FAILURE

British writer Theodore Dalrymple concedes, "It is not as easy as one might suppose to rid oneself of the notion of God."[3] He goes on to describe the darkness in vivid detail. His lack of faith isn't because he's naive to the state of the world; it's his unwillingness to believe there's a light bright enough to drive the dark away.

The medal stand at the 1968 Olympics, the protest at Tiananmen Square, and the fall of the Berlin Wall were profound triumphs, but they were also limited to being just, well, moments. They were little pinpricks of light in a pitch-black room. They were a door creaking open—a blade of light cutting through the blackest dark—and then suddenly slamming shut as quickly as it was opened. They were just moments of light amid long stretches of darkness, brief interruptions. The light is not the rule; it's the exception. The light is a very welcome intrusion, but we are much better acquainted with darkness.

Those athletes raised their fists as a hopeful symbol of a more just future, but the weight of that moment was the product of many, many generations of horrific injustice and dehumanizing wrong. That moment of breakthrough came on the heels of lies about a better life to Africans to get them onto a boat. It followed generations of mistreatment, malnourishment, commodification, torture, and systemic oppression we sum up in the one word—*slavery*. It was one in many painstaking steps up a tall, steep journey called the civil rights movement. It was preceded that very year by the assassination of Martin Luther King Jr., whose only crime was a peaceful stand against systemic racism. Year after year after year of pitch-black darkness, and then a head is bowed, a fist is raised, and the whole world listens and joins the conversation. A door creaked open for a moment, and a blade of light cut the dark. But it was only a moment.

That man who stood against a tank in Tiananmen Square—he was a powerful symbol of courage in the face of oppression. The world watched, and the courage to stand boldly against injustice and tyranny spread into the hearts of many others. That moment was a pinhole of light poked into a box of pitch-black. It took someone living an alternative story so provocatively for just a moment to show a better way, to shed a little light that we might see.

But why did we need such a symbol in the first place? Only because oppression had become the norm in China. Only because the situation had gotten so bad that demonstrations demanding rights had to be organized, and only because the abuse of power had become so corrupt that the solution to opposition was to turn a nation's force on its own people. That profound moment was preceded by year after year after year of darkness. Then a pin poked a hole, and a single ray of light shot in, dust dancing in the beam. But, of course, it was only a moment.

Beethoven's Ninth Symphony was first performed in May 1824. The "Ode to Joy" was an old, famous song. On the night it was played atop the Berlin Wall, there was likely not a soul in the crowd hearing it for the first time. Everyone knew where the song was going; they could hum the big crescendo before the orchestra reached it. So if it wasn't surprise that made this moment leap out of history, what was it?

Why did the whole world get goose bumps during a familiar tune one December night in 1989? Why did so many different people sit in silence, speechless in the best way, when the final note sent invisible sound waves echoing through the air? Only because it was such a dramatic departure from the twenty-eight years' worth of moments that led up to it. Light illuminates recurring darkness only because it's tragically foreign.

The only reason anyone experienced something transcendent that night was because it was like a match struck in a pitch-black room. A match struck at noon on a sunny day gets almost no one's attention; it just blends in. Strike that same match at midnight, though, and it turns the necks of everyone within eyeshot.

The significance of this moment was sadly made possible by all the darkness that crept in for twenty-eight years until no one could see their own hand held up in front of their face. Twenty-eight years before, families were divided by military force. Siblings, cousins, best friends, high school sweethearts, teammates, coworkers—they were all driven apart. Human relationships were severed by a political conflict that couldn't be solved, so it fell like a wedge between the people caught in its path. That wedge drove so deep into the ground that it wouldn't budge for a long, long time.

Then Leonard Bernstein struck a match in the form of Beethoven's Ninth, and all of Germany saw a light pierce the night, smoke dancing above the flame, illuminated by an orb glowing warmly . . . but only for a moment. On this side of Eden, all symphonies remain unfinished.

Triumph isn't decades of darkness that finally give way to a single, fleeting moment of light. Triumph is when that moment is the rule, not the exception. But it isn't. After the medal ceremony and Tiananmen Square and the Philharmonic ringing out over the Berlin Wall, things just retreated back to the same old. The tears behind every eye receded; the hair on the back of every neck lay back down; we pulled ourselves together and resumed life as normal. The match burned out, and our eyes readjusted to the pitch-black dark.

Karl Rahner said it with stinging accuracy: "In the torment

of the insufficiency of everything attainable, we learn that ultimately in this world there is no finished symphony."[4]

In spite of the unfathomable potential of this planet, this life, even just this moment, the straightforward, honest truth is that any objective look back across the human race shows the primary colors shading our history—misuse of power, hoarding of resources, and "taking" by any means necessary.

And that's not a religiously motivated opinion or a particularly cynical read on the state of affairs. That's just honesty, and it's agreed on by every religion, philosophy, system of belief or unbelief, and history book. Darkness haunts our collective best intentions. It always has.

PERSONAL FAILURE

It would be convenient if we could stop there, if we could point the finger at an impersonal force or a faceless other that exists in an abstract social sphere, but we can't, because the darkness is so much more personal than that. History reveals the darkness of the human condition, but we don't even need history. Any human being who has ever taken a long, hard, honest look at their own heart reaches the same conclusion: even our noblest acts are shaded by selfish motives.

Let's go back to that hospital room where my first son was born. The silent celebration shared in that room was real, but it also represents a quickly passing moment of innocence. Even as we fight back tears at the mysterious potential of a new, uncontaminated life, we know the sobering truth. This unformed, uncorrupted, and wholly innocent little living potential will very quickly feel needs and make demands. From the very start, we are creatures of desire, driven by the demand to satisfy our own individual desires.

That wholly innocent little life of potential also has desire burning within it like a small spark. That spark can be kindled into something good, but it can also run wild, bringing destruction and wreaking havoc on anyone and everyone in its path. C. S. Lewis writes, "From the moment a creature becomes aware of God as God and of itself as self, the terrible alternative of choosing God or the self for the centre is opened to it."[5]

Every injustice, every oppression, every imbalanced society started when someone, somewhere put themselves at the center of the story and demanded cooperation from the rest of us. There are big and small ways we do this—socially tragic examples like American racism, Chinese oppression, or German division, all of which started with individuals who chose the self for the center—but there are smaller examples too. There is such a thing as living selfishly while maintaining the subtlety that keeps your name out of the history books. Choosing the self for the center can and does look like racism, oppression, and violence, but it also looks like day after day in a world where all those things are present but being so caught up in "my thing" that I do nothing consequential about it. Choosing the self for the center also looks like allowing my career, my appearance, or my definition of success to sit on the throne of my life and rule. Choosing the self for the center sometimes looks like immoral action, and other times it looks like apathy that silently cooperates with those actions. Both ingredients are necessary for a world that can't seem to push back the dark.

A picture may be helpful. I was standing on the subway platform at Bedford Avenue in New York City. It was a midmorning in early summer, and I was daydreaming about vacation— freedom from responsibility and complete relaxation. I traveled to Greece for a week in college, and that's the most magical place I've been, so I was going back there in my imagination.

I see myself sitting at a café table eating lunch, where every flavor was so bright and so loud. I thought I had tasted olives and feta before . . . I hadn't. I remember hanging my feet over the harbor, where cliffs dive straight into the Mediterranean. I can almost feel the steps I walked through Athens, sipping coffee with the locals.

But I also remember stepping into a tourist trap gift shop near the Parthenon. You can buy postcards with black and white photos from the 1940s, when Greece was completely occupied by German forces. When the café where I ate lunch might have been barracks where soldiers slept. The beautiful harbor I hung my feet over was likely a parking lot for fighter planes. Those locals I sipped coffee with—the ones old enough to have lived through it—would have lived in constant fear. The place I go in my daydreams is also the place some go in their nightmares.

Think about the soldiers enforcing all that—going into someone's home, looking them in the eye, and then taking their culture, their safety, their livelihood, their future, ultimately their dignity. Those soldiers were born just like you and me— innocent, unformed, wide-eyed little babies full of potential. Normal people. How can ordinary human beings, put into a particular situation, do such monstrous things?[6]

I guess, looking back across history, we have to admit there are dark spots where primitive human impulses were allowed to rule. But we are "progressive" people, right? We—those of us reading books like this one—are too sophisticated for that sort of thing, aren't we?

I snapped out of that vacation daydream because I could see the subway train approaching. And as it did, a nervous frenzy ran over the crowded platform, and everyone started implementing their strategy. Some people started guessing where the doors would be and claiming their spot. Others used their enormous backpacks as leverage against the weak. The last person to walk down the steps subtly slipped ahead of the rest and onto the yellow track like he'd been waiting for fifteen minutes. This is the L train to Manhattan at 9:00 a.m. It's a silent battle.

Not everyone's getting on that subway car, so every normal, innocent person is overtaken by the same thought at the same time: *I'm too important to wait for the next one.*

From 9:00 to 10:00 a.m., Monday through Friday, a bunch of sophisticated, progressive New Yorkers are owned by those same "primitive instincts." We dress them up most of the time, but when there's space for one and it's me or you . . . something comes out of us.

Buy a postcard at a gift shop in Athens, and you'll be confronted by the spotty history of the human race. Go to work tomorrow morning in New York City, and you'll be confronted by the spotty present of the human race.

STRANDS OF SIN

The most effective strands of this debilitating disease called sin are not the obvious ills. An American slave owner running a plantation like a tyrant, a Chinese government limiting quality of life for the sake of control, German politicians chopping up a city—these are easy to recognize, rendering them less effective. The contagious strands, the ones that ravage a population so completely that health is the exception, are the convincing counterfeits. It's the human attempts to mend the open, infected wounds of this world by our best intentions, the subconscious belief that what plagues our world is simple enough that it can be solved through a generation or two of well-intentioned people. It's the human attempt to pull a full, satisfying, complete life into being by our own resources—to find deep meaning, lasting peace, and soul-level fulfillment apart from God.

Sin is meeting the deep needs of my life by my own resources.[7] Good intentions powered by human resources bring more pain than healing. That's the strand of sin that has infected most of us. The mission is so right, but the method is so destructive.

Richard Dawkins, the world's most famous atheist, builds his unbelief on a premise called "the selfish gene," set forth in his 1976 book by the same title.[8] In summary, Dawkins isn't claiming that human beings are selfish at the level of our will or motives. No, no, it's much deeper and darker than that. His premise is that the DNA that survives and is passed on is the more self-interested strand. The "selfish gene" always wins. In other words, there is no real service, no real kindness, no real love. There's only self-interest, and everything you and I do is for self-promotion. You can't help it, and neither can I. It's our DNA. As history rolls on, it only gets worse.

While I adamantly disagree with Dawkins on all of this, I respect his honesty on this point: We are conveniently fooling ourselves if we think the problem can be summed up as "the world is in need of fixing." That's true, but it only gets us halfway home. The whole truth is that I am in need of fixing, and so are you. I am haunted by a recurring darkness from within, not only from without, and so are you. As psychologist David Benner so pointedly wrote, "It is not so much that we tell lies as that we live them."[9]

This is where the common modern Western understanding splits from the biblical story. Everyone believes in a flawed world, but some think that cosmetic repairs to the exterior will do. Christians believe our world is flawed to the core, that the wreckage is beyond a wrench or a brush. Some subconsciously imagine the world's been in a fender bender; the biblical claim is that it's totaled.

My favorite definition of sin isn't found in Genesis. It comes from a letter from the apostle Paul to a few small house churches meeting in first-century Rome:

> They exchanged the truth about God for a lie, and worshiped and served created things rather than the Creator.
>
> *Romans 1:25*

Exchange God (the Creator) with anyone or anything else (a created thing), and you may feel liberated and free for a moment, but that new center is taking you somewhere. Is it somewhere you want to go?

In her memoir titled *Educated,* Tara Westover comes to terms with her dysfunctional relationship with her brother: "He had defined me to myself, and there's no greater power than that."[10] That's the rub of the human condition—rebellion against God doesn't equal autonomous freedom; it equals a substitute god. Something else, something outside of myself, has to define me to myself. When sin took that defining power from God, it didn't hand it over to me. It handed it to some other outside source— someone or something outside of me. Who or what defines you to yourself? That's where the power in your life lies. That's your new king and the one you worship.

The award-winning novelist David Foster Wallace said this best in a commencement speech to a roomful of college graduates:

> In the day-to-day trenches of adult life, there is actually no such thing as atheism. There is no such thing as not worshipping. Everybody worships. The only choice we get is *what* to worship. And an outstanding reason for choosing some sort of God or spiritual-type thing to worship . . . is that pretty much anything else you worship will eat you alive . . . If you worship money and things—if they are where you tap real meaning in life—then you will never have enough. Never feel you have enough. It's the truth. Worship your own body and beauty and sexual allure and you will always feel ugly, and when time and age start showing, you will die a million deaths before they finally plant you . . . Worship power—you will feel weak and afraid, and you will need ever more power over others to keep the fear at bay. Worship your intellect,

being seen as smart—you will end up feeling stupid, a fraud, always on the verge of being found out.[11]

Is there anyone, anywhere who isn't exposed by those words? Point the finger at a world in need of fixing without also being honest about the unique ways you've chosen some created thing to be the center of your life, and you're only deceiving yourself. Something—consumption, power, success, beauty, desirability, image—is sitting at the center of your life, being asked to deliver meaning, to be enough, to tell you you're enough. Something good becomes something ultimate, and when that something is any created thing rather than the Creator, it "will eat you alive." That's sin, but of course, you can give it a different name if you prefer.

DRINKING DIRTY WATER

There's a particularly poignant image used by the prophet Jeremiah, who, looking around at his world, shows us that not a lot has changed in the last few thousand years: "My people have committed two sins: They have forsaken me, the spring of living water, and have dug their own cisterns, broken cisterns that cannot hold water" (Jeremiah 2:13).

This picture creates a vivid image of the two steps we all know so personally.

"My people have committed two sins: They have forsaken me, the spring of living water . . ." First, God has been removed from the center. I did not choose when to be born, where to be born, who my family would be, what my race would be—and the list could go on and on. All the evidence points to one conclusion: I am not the author. I entered someone else's story by someone else's will. Whether you believe this someone is an intelligent designer, a powerful but impersonal force, a scientific accident, or something else is another question entirely. What the evidence proves conclusively is this: I have such little control over my life. To push God out of the center is also to reach for the control that I lack. It is an attempt to snatch the pen from the author's hand—to write the script, direct the film, and play the lead all at the same time. Russell Moore, reaching all the way back to the Genesis story, calls Adam and Eve's temptation a playbook for our own: "You will be tempted to provide for yourself, to protect yourself, and to exalt yourself. And at the core of these three is a common impulse—to cast off the fatherhood of God."[12]

". . . and have dug their own cisterns, broken cisterns that cannot hold water." The center of our lives never remains vacant, so we put something else there. We dig our own wells, draw our own water, and try to quench our own thirst. This "well digging" can be expressed in endlessly unique varieties: You try to satisfy the deepest longings of the human condition through a particular socioeconomic status you're convinced will result in contentment. Or you've talked yourself into a degree of power that will make you feel the ground under your two feet—that elusive feeling called control. Or regardless of what you say, your life says you believe a clear complexion and a photoshop-quality body can make you desirable enough to actually feel desirable. It could be some accumulation of career success that will allow you to rest, to say, *There. Now that's enough. Now I'll put my feet up on my desk and enjoy the fruits of my labor.* Pick your poison. Dig your well. Draw your choice of water.

Prior to the Enlightenment, people obsessed over an assumed eternity that must lie beyond this temporary life. Today, people obsess over squeezing eternity into this temporary life. We dig one cistern after another, thinking that with enough different water sources to draw from, we can do the impossible—we can find fulfillment on our own terms.

Sin has never been about moral guidelines, because the issue is not that you're too thirsty; the issue is that you're drinking from the wrong well. Monsignor Lorenzo Albacete wrote, "There is only one temptation. All particular temptations are expressions of this one original or 'primordial' temptation. This is the temptation to believe that the fulfillment of the desires of the human heart depends entirely on us."[13]

At the midpoint of a long, hot day in the Middle Eastern desert, Jesus sat down on the rim of a well. He struck up an interesting conversation with a woman who had come to draw water there. Here's the memorable line from their dialogue:

> "Everyone who drinks this water will be thirsty again, but whoever drinks the water I give them will never thirst. Indeed, the water I give them will become in them a spring of water welling up to eternal life."
>
> *John 4:13–14*

Jesus was essentially quoting Jeremiah. He was saying to this woman (and to all who would listen), "How many times will you stumble dehydrated toward the wells you dug for yourself before you finally admit you're still thirsty?"

Jesus picked up the same theme in John 7:

> On the last and greatest day of the festival, Jesus stood and said in a loud voice, "Let anyone who is thirsty come to me and drink. Whoever believes in me, as Scripture has said, rivers of living water will flow from within them."
>
> *John 7:37–38*

"The festival" Jesus was attending was the Festival of Tabernacles, an annual Jewish holiday. In ancient times, it was a well-attended pilgrimage festival, meaning the Jewish people traveled from every corner of Israel to fill the city of Jerusalem for a weeklong celebration. During this particular festival, all the people lived in handmade tabernacles (the Hebrew equivalent of a tent). An entire country descends on a single city and camps for a seven-day festival. It was the Coachella of ancient Israel.

During the Festival of Tabernacles, all would gather for the daily temple ritual. The priests would pour a cistern of water down the temple steps, symbolic of the river of God's Spirit that the prophet Ezekiel envisioned flowing out of the temple,[14] as the massive crowd sang the psalms in unison. All of this built anticipation for the final day, when the priests poured seven cisterns of water down the temple steps, creating a visible stream flowing from the temple into the streets.

This was day seven. The celebration is reaching the climactic moment as all of Israel carried the same tune and the ornate priests methodically drenched the sacred steps. That's when Jesus, uninvited, joined them on the steps and screamed loud enough to bring the whole thing to a standstill: "Let anyone who is thirsty come to me and drink. Whoever believes in me, as Scripture has said, rivers of living water will flow from within them."

"It is hard to get enough of something that *almost* works."[15] That's the observation of Dr. Vincent Felitti, commenting on the power that addiction holds over his patients. We have a hard time resisting that same old polluted water from that same old man-made well because it *almost* works. Escaping my problems into substance or sex or pornography almost works. Finding value in success or desirability or attention *almost* works. The pursuit of more possessions or comforts or the endless allure of upgrades *almost* works. A new adventure, new job, new spouse, new city to still the choppy waters of my inner discontent *almost* works. Our thirst is quenched for a moment, but it's a fleeting moment, and with diminishing returns.

Our "broken cisterns" are filled with saltwater—soothing to the surface of our dry tongues but, at a deeper, truer level, killing us with every sip. So again, Jesus invites us, "Let anyone who is thirsty come to me and drink."

PAY ATTENTION

You can read the Bible to make the critical observation of sin within yourself, but you can reach the same conclusion just by paying attention.

The recurring darkness of our world can't just be pinned on some unseen, unnamed, abstract forces out there somewhere, because every last one of us can quickly picture the face of someone somewhere who has let us down personally. It doesn't take long for the face of someone who has wounded us, maybe in ways we are still recovering from, to come to mind. That face, the one you get knots of anxiety churning in your gut just thinking about, was once celebrated as a new life of unfathomable potential—unformed, uncorrupted, uncontaminated, and wholly innocent. But it didn't take long for that innocent life to feel need and start making demands. You are the collateral of those demands.

And here's the harder pill to swallow—that face is you and it's me in the imagination of someone else. You were once celebrated as an unformed, uncorrupted, uncontaminated, wholly innocent life with nothing but potential. But it didn't take long for you to feel need and start making demands. There's real collateral to those demands, collateral with a face and a name and a story.

There are such far-reaching consequences to this impulse to put the self at the center.

Every origin story, philosophy, and religion must confront this indisputable fact: something has gone wrong with the human race. The denial of darkness doesn't take the darkness away;

it just keeps you stumbling around in the same darkness with your eyes closed. G. K. Chesterton, in his seminal work explaining his own faith, calls "original sin" the only part of Christian theology that can really be proved.[16]

The narrator of the novel *Gilead* says it with startling honesty: "If you want to inform yourselves as to the nature of hell, don't hold your hand in a candle flame, just ponder the meanest, most desolate place in your [own] soul."[17]

That's a fictional tale, though, dreamed up only in the imagination. Famed psychologist Viktor Frankl lived in the real-life tension of this stark reality. Not only was he a Jew living during the WWII era; he was also a prisoner in Auschwitz—observing the conditions of a concentration camp as both a doctor and a victim himself. Somehow surviving the horror, he wrote a masterpiece titled *Man's Search for Meaning*, applying objective expertise to his subjective experience. Here are the final words of his original manuscript, stunningly sober and hopeful at the same time:

> Our generation is realistic, for we have come to know man as he really is. After all, man is that being who invented the gas chambers of Auschwitz; however, he is also that being who entered those gas chambers upright, with the Lord's Prayer or the *Shema Yisrael* on his lips.[18]

CHAPTER FOUR

ABRUPT ENDING

"S o do you really think there's a heaven or hell on the other side of all this?" He blurted it out before I'd even rested my full weight on the stool. Not even a hello. That's a surprising way to get to know someone. I'd never had a real conversation with Joey before, though he explained he'd been coming to our church services sporadically for a couple months. Before I had a chance to respond to his question, he filled the pause with the backstory.

Joey moved to New York City years before as a musician. He was a percussionist with a taste for punk rock, so he made his way from suburban Ohio to the birthplace of punk as soon as he could scrounge together enough cash. Years later, his nights were still spent gigging around with a few different bands on the local scene, and his days managing a few different rehearsal spaces. His days were spent in proximity to music, and his nights were all fun and adventure. He loved it.

Then, quite suddenly, his father died.

He flew back home, paid his respects, and watched as a Catholic priest he had never met said a few words to sum up the life of the man who raised Joey. His father's body lay in a casket, absent of the personality and sense of humor that had always filled it. The arms that made Joey feel safe as a little boy, the voice he can still hear when he closes his eyes, the little mannerisms he accidentally imitates—all of that gone. Just a lifeless body he both recognized and didn't at the same time, and a whole life summed up in a few phrases.

Joey came back to New York after that, but his fun, free, adventurous life had lost its luster. His world of color had faded to black-and-white. Grief has a way of draining the light out of everything. So here he sat, at thirty-eight, across from the pastor of the only church he'd ever willingly attended, fighting tears, asking a relative stranger, "Do you think there's a chance that when the last breath left my dad's lungs, he might've experienced some kind of relief?"

THE INEVITABILITY OF DEATH

There is an inevitable point at which every single person is confronted by the recurring darkness that looms over life's potential. Even the person most committed to ignoring what's right in front of them, the person refusing to pay attention, will be grabbed one day by both cheeks and forced to stare the darkness right in the face in their final breaths. I'm talking about death. I'm talking about the fact we eventually can't ignore no matter how hard we try. You are going to die. Every life will one day come to an abrupt ending.

The darkness of this world is never so apparent as in the moment of death. We don't like to think about that. We defer that knowledge almost every moment of our waking lives, but it's the one thing I share with every reader of this book: you are going to die, and so am I.

In the ancient world, large cities had a separate township built beyond the city's border called a *necropolis*, which, translated into English, means "city of the dead." Cemeteries were large enough to possess their own zip code, and in some cases, the law prevented anyone from burying a body within the proper city limits. Whole societies found a way to live that avoided the inevitability of death.

In the modern world, we've continued the trend. Western

culture celebrates youth and has found endless ways to prolong it through age-defying makeup, dietary supplements, and cosmetic surgery. And when the end is finally so close that we can't deny it anymore, we enlist professionals—assisted living facilities for the elderly, hospitals for life's final breaths, and morgues to make the deceased look presentable.

According to research conducted by American Senior Communities, more than one million Americans currently live in assisted living facilities, and that number is expected to double by 2030.[1] In many cases, these are great homes staffed by extraordinary people, but the numbers reveal the new and growing trend that the elderly are cared for not by their families in the final years as their bodies break down but by hired professionals.

According to Stanford medical research, 60 percent of Americans die in hospitals, and another 20 percent take their last breath in a nursing home. This leaves only 20 percent who die at home—their own or that of a loved one.[2] Is it a better alternative to die at home? The same study reveals that 80 percent of the polled elderly would prefer to die at home, but preference is beside the point. These stats clearly reveal that modern society is shielded from intimate interaction with death in a historically unprecedented way. We've done our very best to insulate ourselves from the fact of our own expiration, turning death into an industry handled by professionals.

It wasn't too long ago that the elderly lived with families, died in homes, and were prepared for remembrance by their loved ones. For most of history, people have been much more acquainted with death than we are today. People have lived with death, participated in death, been forced to confront death before it was their own.

Humanity has never stopped inventing new ways of pretending that life goes on forever, but, of course, the stark truth is that you are going to die. And on that day, it won't matter how trendy the furniture is in your new apartment, how good you look with your shirt off, what title is next to your name on LinkedIn, or how important you are when you walk into a particular room. A life ignorant of death is not more free, but less free. To quote Ernest Becker, who brilliantly summarized the psychology of modern relationship to death, "The result was the emergence of man as we know him: a hyperanxious animal who constantly invents reasons for anxiety even when there are none."[3]

We're not the necropolis, but passing our days in denial of our own expiration lives on. Though we've found a way of living that lets us forget it most of the time, death is an inevitability, which may make its sting all the more abrupt.

THREE FAMILIES

In the last year, I've sat with three families from the church I pastor, grieving the loss of loved ones under the age of forty.

Juan

I'll never forget walking into Woodhull Medical Center in Brooklyn. It was standing room only. One Puerto Rican family had shown up en masse, filling every seat in the waiting room—mother, father, siblings, cousins, aunts, uncles, grandparents, and children. They were all there, trying to make sense of a suicide no one had seen coming. A young man—mid-thirties, a son, brother, and father—locked himself in his apartment bathroom one Saturday morning in early spring and swallowed a lethal dose of pills. I searched everywhere for the right thing to say. I wanted so desperately to have a few words that would strike a match of light in that pitch-black room, but everything that ran through my imagination to say seemed hollow against the weight of the moment. I offered a short prayer and just sat in the pain, suffocated by the injustice smothering the room. I took the long way home that night, pedaling my bike as slowly as I could while keeping it upright. There's no hurry to resume ordinary life when you've sat under the loom of recurring darkness.

Jade

I got the text midmorning. A close friend had just found out that her older sister had a bad enough case of the flu that she had to go to the hospital. That happened to me once. For a second, I was transported back to a nausea debilitating enough that I had to go to the ER to get some fluids. I shook off the bad memory, prayed a quick prayer for a woman I had never met but now felt confident I shared a bad experience with, and got back to work.

A couple of days later, she was gone. A forty-year-old mother of two—completely healthy, less than a week removed from a New Year's Eve night out with friends—had died from an airborne virus. How can that be? How can you be laughing and toasting and making resolutions toward another year, with no indication that you don't have time to live those resolutions or experience the future you're looking forward to?

Early January had brought a blizzard to New York. It always seems to happen like that. The cold weather is exciting when it's accompanied by Christmas lights and office parties, but then early January greets the whole city with the harsh reality that winter has three more months to go, in a good year. We sat in a warm apartment, passing paper containers of Indian food around the kitchen table. No one said much. There wasn't much to say. Jade's sister was gone, and it was still so fresh that the grief probably wouldn't really set in for a few more days. So, as her friends, we just sat with her in the shock of it all. We prayed, and our prayers were honest. They had a lot more questions than answers in them.

My apartment is only a block away, but I walked a long way

that night, watching the snow fall in the streetlights, piling up on top of the cars. I didn't talk to myself or to God very much. I didn't mull over questions or try to make sense of it. I just felt the darkness, walked around carrying its weight on my back. Moving on felt cheap after I was confronted with how fragile life really is.

Jayson

I sat in a home with three generations of the Wilshusen family while Jayson, a guy in his late twenties, lay deceased on the couch. That's where he was found. He had been out of prison for less than twenty-four hours when, after a nearly lifelong battle with addiction, he overdosed. His mother hadn't even gotten to see him yet. It took hours for the coroner and morgue attendant to arrive. It was a small apartment, so his body—lifeless, cold, exposed—remained in plain view for everyone to see—mother, brother, grandmother, and a few close friends. Thankfully, his four-year-old daughter was living with her mother a state away. After a few prayers and a lot of tears, the questions everyone was thinking but didn't have the strength to ask hung in the air.

I went straight from there to a child's birthday party. As I celebrated with one family, I couldn't help but think about the other. Two mothers who shared a faith, a city, a community, living just a mile apart. One celebrating the life of her son, while another mourned the loss of hers.

I lay awake that night, thinking about all those questions that hung silently in the air that day. All those questions that were still stuck to me while I sang happy birthday to a three-year-old. All those unshakable questions that the finality of death—that thing we've mastered distracting ourselves from—forces on us all of a sudden. It forced itself on me that day, and it would release its grip soon so I could return to my life of distraction. But I wasn't ready to wriggle out of its grip just yet. I didn't have the strength.

AM I DYING?

In July 2014, I heard a five-minute TED talk that I've probably spent five thousand minutes turning over in my mind. It wasn't given by a polished developer or researcher used to giving presentations on "groundbreaking innovations" that you (you being a crowd of wealthy investors playing real-life Monopoly against one another) are invited to get in on the ground floor of.

These were five jittery minutes, the first few sentences coming out hurried as the presenter fidgeted through nervous tics. The words were backed by a New York accent that is becoming something of an endangered species in the city I call home. It's a relic of the past—what the outer boroughs used to be in a previous, more romantic era.

Matthew O'Reilly is an EMT first responder in Suffolk County, Long Island. His five-minute talk was titled "Am I Dying?"[4] The subject of his talk was a moral dilemma common to EMTs. He often arrives at the scene of some horrible event, only to realize that he is standing over someone who is breathing their final breaths, with nothing he or any other medical professional can do for them. At that point, the suffering person will often ask, "Am I dying?" That leaves two bad options open to him: he can lie, keeping hope intact, even though there's nothing to actually hope in, or he can tell the truth, delivering the worst news of all to a complete stranger.

For years, O'Reilly did what I imagine most EMTs do. He lied. He looked into the eyes of the dying, so far beyond hope that even attempting medical intervention was too late, and said, "No, you're not going to die today. Hang in there." All he could do was watch for the next few seconds as their eyes rolled back in their head.

One day, he surprised himself. Arriving on the scene of a brutal motorcycle accident, he rushed out of the ambulance and kneeled down over the top of the rider, whose body was splayed out on the pavement. Quickly, O'Reilly assessed that nothing could be done for this man who was moments from everything going dark, when the man asked that familiar question: "Am I going to die?" In a shocking need to be honest, to let this accident victim hear the truth and make of it what he wanted, O'Reilly said, "Yes. You're going to die. There's nothing I can do for you." The reaction wasn't the terror he feared. Something felt right about letting the dying at least know they're dying. In some small way, he could make the ending a bit less abrupt.

From that day on, he was done lying to the doomed. The truth was less comfortable but more dignifying. In the years since, he's kept on with the truth, observing three common patterns experienced by those aware that they're walking the final steps between their journey in this world and the great unknown: the need for forgiveness, the need for remembrance, and the need to know their life had meaning.

When the final page of a single life is written, every human being this medical technician has ever stood over has expressed regret. Awareness of personal wrong and regret for the ripple effects of that wrong in the lives of others are universal. It cuts across every variety of belief and unbelief. In O'Reilly's own words, "The first pattern always kind of shocked me. Regardless of religious belief or cultural background, there's a need for forgiveness. Whether they call it sin or they simply say they have a regret, guilt is universal."

I have a three-year-old son and have watched the Pixar movie *Coco* more than anything of my own choosing in the last six months. As embarrassing as it may be to admit, I find one piece of the plot to be profound. In the movie, when the living die, they go to the land of the dying, which is more like an amusement park than a haunted house, so stop judging me for watching this with a toddler. But, and here's the part with a profound kernel of existential truth, the land of the dying, even in the dream world of Pixar screenwriters, is not the final destination. You live on there until you're completely forgotten. The day you're no longer alive in the memory of any living person, you die a second and, seemingly final, death.

"Will anyone remember me?" That's the next question EMTs watch race through the minds of the dying. There's a universal need for remembrance, which everyone reaches out for when the end is closing in on them. Every human being, when faced with death, has an instinctive desire for something eternal, an instinctive desire to keep living, even if only in the memory of others.

"There was so much more I wanted to do with my life." Lying next to crumpled metal and spilled oil, a growing pool of blood forming underneath a failing body, the final thing that passes through the consciousness of the dying is the people, the places, the dreams, and the experiences. The people I gave everything to and those I wish I had given more. The places I passed my time, the places I should've spent more time in, and the places I wasted far too much time in. The dreams I brought to life and lived—were they as good in my life as they seemed to be in my imagination? The dreams that never made the jump from imagination to reality—were the forces that kept them hidden worth it? Then finally the collection of experiences that made up my days, which at one time felt endless and now suddenly seem unjustly short. "Was this enough? Did any of this really, truthfully matter? Did I matter?" There are no sentimental answers to these questions in life's final breath. You face them with stark, brutal honesty, maybe for the first time.

IS THERE ANYTHING I HAVE THAT DEATH CANNOT TAKE?

Some people face ultimate questions before their final breaths though. They're either the bravest or most morbid among us, and I'm really not sure which. Leo Tolstoy looked long and hard into his own mortality and then put his brutally honest thoughts on paper:

> My question—that which at the age of fifty brought me to the verge of suicide—was the simplest of questions, lying in the soul of every man from the foolish child to the wisest elder: it was a question without an answer . . . It was: "What will come of what I am doing today or shall do tomorrow? What will come of my whole life?"
>
> Differently expressed, the question is . . . "Is there any meaning in my life that the inevitable death awaiting me does not destroy?"[5]

No one gets to ignore this question. Every individual life has to ask it, but so does the entire cosmos as we know it. Scientists have universally arrived at the conclusion that the universe is expanding, growing farther and farther apart, getting colder and colder. Eventually every star will burn out. All matter will collapse. All light, all heat, all life will disappear, leaving only cold, hard matter eternally expanding into space, far too cold to sustain any kind of life. The universe, based on every scientific discovery, is going to die.[6]

Peer through the lens of a microscope or the lens of a telescope, and what you see is going to die. The wonder of the cosmos you used to slow down enough to admire every once in a while and the atoms your middle school science teacher taught you actually make up everything you can see and touch on the most fundamental, microscopic level—it's all dying. Just look up from reading this book and take a look at the people, the life, the matter you see all around you; just look at your own reflection in the mirror. Everything you see, everyone you see—as far as your eye can see—is going to die.

In his book *The Denial of Death*, Ernest Becker writes, "All historical religions addressed themselves to this same problem of how to bear the end of life . . . When philosophy took over from religion it also took over religion's central problem and death became the real 'muse of philosophy.'"[7] French philosopher Luc Ferry said it more succinctly: "All philosophy throughout history is trying to deal with one thing: Death."[8]

Tolstoy, leaning back from his typewriter, pipe clenched in his teeth; the ambitious scientist with a wall full of degrees; the ten-year-old leukemia patient in that most sobering wing of the hospital; the elderly matriarch whose heart is failing after an objectively long and full life; the victim of a motorcycle accident spread out motionless on the pavement, shaded by the silhouette of a stranger in uniform—they're all asking the same question: *Is there anything I have that death cannot take?*

That's the question we manage to spend the vast majority of our days ignoring and the question that every abrupt ending forces us to face, at least for a moment. We are the recipients or architects (or maybe both) of a society that has pushed our own expiration as far from human consciousness as possible, but occasionally we remember the inevitable ending of it all for a moment.

Is there anything I have—any possession, experience, memory, legacy, hope, intention, relationship, anything at all—that the inevitable death awaiting me will not destroy?

CHAPTER FIVE

AN ORDINARY TUESDAY AFTERNOON

There you have it: *the story of the world.*

The whole thing, every huge, sweeping theme summarized as an era, documented in history books, and memorized by mostly uninterested students for history tests; every endlessly deep but painfully short human life; every tiny moment happening simultaneously in seven and a half billion human lives right now—all of it. It all plays out between two opposing forces: unfathomable potential and recurring darkness.

You can rename these forces if you want. They've been renamed in civilization and philosophy, dating as far back as we can reach. The rock and hard place that I'm calling potential and darkness—that's where we live, wedged right between the two.

And all of that inevitably brings us to an ordinary Tuesday afternoon.

Because anytime now, your train of thought is going to be broken by a crying baby or an email from your micromanaging boss or the need to pee. In other words, any serious thought about human life has to eventually get down to the nitty-gritty of human life. Anything that really matters has to really matter on ordinary Tuesday afternoons.

So here you are, inserted as a character into a story you didn't author, a story that was being written long before you became aware of it and will go on being written long after you leave

61

it. Here you are, experiencing the unfathomable potential of this life while also occasionally being reminded of the nagging, inescapable reality of recurring darkness. Or maybe it's the other way around. For you, it's the darkness of this world that is most obvious, and you occasionally get a splash of the very good potential, like a single ray of sunshine that breaks, for just a moment, through dark clouds on a gloomy day.

The limited days of our lives are wedged between these two forces, so how do we live on an ordinary Tuesday afternoon? The way I see it, we are always choosing between two options: either we fight the darkness or change the subject.

FIGHT THE DARKNESS

Do not go gentle into that good night . . .
Rage, rage against the dying of the light.

I don't believe it's ever been said more pointedly or clearly than Dylan Thomas put it in his famous poem "Do Not Go Gentle into That Good Night." There is a certain sort of person who lives like Thomas did—on a pilgrimage for answers to the foundational questions. I have to admit a deep respect for this sort of living—an appetite for deep thought, hours of conversation and debate, endless reading from both the greats and the forgotten, this perspective and that.

Countless philosophers have spent their entire lives asking question after question in search of satisfying answers, raging against the dying of the light. We benefit from their work. But of course, the dying light did catch up to them, like all the rest. That's not to discredit the very sincere search. It's just to admit that in the end, they lost the fight.

Elon Musk is doing his best to build us all another world to go on living in. He's fighting the dying light, raging against his own mortality, and probably doing it with more forthright honesty than the rest of us, who fight much more secretly and quietly. But, of course, the dying light will catch up to him and me and you. In the end, we will lose the fight.

Dylan Thomas lost the fight. He lived more in thirty-nine years than most people squeeze into twice that. He dropped out of school to focus on writing at sixteen, moved to London as a poet at twenty, grew in acclaim from his books and on-air radio readings so quickly that in his twenties his name was being mentioned alongside T. S. Eliot and W. H. Auden. He was one of the best. He was a prodigy. His whole life was out ahead of him. *Potential* is the word for it, and he was fighting the darkness.

He did his first of four reading tours in America when he was thirty-five to much critical acclaim and significant growth in notoriety and sales. He was scratching and clawing for answers to the most important questions, and his search was put into words that spoke to such a deep place in the soul, a place most didn't (and probably don't) have the courage to go to on their own. He fell in love and got married. He had a baby daughter. His career had taken off on a scale that must have been beyond what even he imagined.

But all of his scratching and clawing wasn't getting him any closer to what he was looking for. The literary empire he was building wasn't doing anything to address the core question at the center of his, and every, human life. So he spent his days writing and his nights drinking. Until, eventually, he spent his days drinking and his nights drinking. On his fourth American tour, with his wife and daughter back in London, Thomas collapsed in the Chelsea Hotel on 23rd St. in Manhattan. He had stumbled and weaved down the crowded sidewalk with the sort of buzz that makes the most serious drinker stagger. Eventually, the biology got the best of him. The alcohol in his bloodstream was stronger than his iron will, and he hit the floor. He was pronounced dead four days later at St. Vincent's Hospital. It was anything but quiet, but he did go into that dark night. It was tragically abrupt, and it was an ending. The light faded and faded until the darkness won.

Fighting the darkness is the first response to mortality recorded in Scripture. Genesis 11 details the construction of the Tower of Babel:

> "Come, let us build ourselves a city, with a tower that reaches to the heavens, so that we may make a name for ourselves; otherwise we will be scattered over the face of the whole earth."
>
> *Genesis 11:4*

There's quite a bit of significance behind the phrase "make a name for ourselves." In ancient Hebrew culture, a name carried much, much more significance than it does in the modern West. A name told a story. It spoke a person's identity. Throughout the Bible, names are frequently changed to signify a particularly formative encounter with the Creator himself—Abraham, Sarah, Jacob, Joshua, and Peter having experienced this, to name a few.

The quest to "make a name for ourselves" was the quest for self-sufficiency. It was the quest to solve the mortality problem on their own. People banded together to build the Tower of Babel, a project to push back the darkness, the original quest for transcendence, but the lives of every last one of its conspirators ended abruptly. The darkness won. They didn't go quietly, but they went.

Jesus once posed this question: "Who of you by worrying can add a single hour to your life?"[1] In other words, whose rage against the consuming darkness has ever been successful in the slightest? The quest is a noble one, but if this quest doesn't end in surrender, it will end in defeat. The darkness is undefeated.

And while I admit a great respect for the courage of the fighter, for those with a stomach for confronting the most sizable questions, only a dwindling fraction of us belong to that group.

The industrialized Western world is an adult amusement park filled with rides and distractions and treats for our consumption. It's a museum of distraction, and so that's how most of us pass our Tuesday afternoons between unfathomable potential and recurring darkness: We change the subject.

CHANGE THE SUBJECT

An ad campaign was launched in London in 2009, funded by a couple of atheist groups who were fed up with all the cheesy evangelical advertising around town. It showed up on eight hundred city buses that April, reading, "There's Probably No God. Now Stop Worrying and Enjoy Your Life."[2]

© Jonathan Hordle / Shutterstock

This is advice most modern people have taken, and it's easy to see why. The world is pretty good. In fact, it's objectively better than it's ever been, so there's plenty to distract yourself with—to keep the big questions from interrupting a perfectly suitable Tuesday afternoon. So just relax. You're probably not on the verge of a breakthrough anyway. If there is some Creator to appease, what are the odds any of us know anything about that cosmic Being? Might as well just do your best to enjoy the few days you've got as much as you possibly can.

Actually, that's not a new idea. A long time before you could find it on the side of public transportation in England, a similar message was frequently found chiseled into rock in Israel. During the lifetime of Jesus, a tombstone inscription so popular that archaeologists have uncovered it in both Greek and Latin read, "I was not. I was. I am not. I don't care."[3] Who knows what this life is or where it came from? Here's what we can agree on: it'll be over one day, so you might as well chill out with the spiritual search and enjoy the best of the distraction.

The story of the world puts every one of us in a troubling predicament. We are forced to live out our days wedged between the beauty and goodness of unfathomable potential and the stark, looming reality of recurring darkness. So I guess we could obsess over the predicament, but we could also just take the advice of secularist thinker Richard John Neuhaus:

> Make it up as you go along; take ironic delight in the truth that there is no truth; there is no home that answers to our homelessness; definitely (but light-heartedly!) throw the final vocabulary that is your life in the face of nothingness. And if your neighbor or some inner curiosity persists in asking about the meaning of it all, simply change the subject.[4]

Honestly, that works most of the time. Changing the subject can get you through most Tuesdays. Distraction is the way the masses get through life. The chosen forms of distraction differ, based on culture and class, but the vast majority of us prefer to throw out the final vocabulary and laugh at another sarcastic joke, to put this book down and pull up our Netflix queue, to keep changing the subject.

Changing the subject works particularly well when life is full of hope and promise. When you've got something to look forward to, you can set pretty much anything else aside. When you're a newlywed or a new parent or have started a new job, or if you've just got plans this weekend, the ultimate questions of life are easily deferred in the name of a simpler, closer subject. When the potential is more apparent, we can dismiss the darkness.

"Stop worrying and enjoy your life" may fit satisfyingly into a life that's on an assumed upward trajectory, but it stops fitting very quickly when pain interrupts our plans, crashing into a future we thought was promised. When marriage becomes divorce, when parents are forced to grieve the loss of a child, when the promising career path ends in termination, or just when weekend plans are traded for idle loneliness, "enjoy your life" isn't a fun distraction anymore. It's insultingly cheap and existentially impossible. When darkness is more apparent than potential, changing the subject isn't enough.

The big moments of life, the ones that stop us because the plans that seemed so secure are revealed to be so fragile; the moments that change us because no one walks through this and comes out the other side quite the same—those kind of moments startle us with the sudden realization: it's not enough.

It's not enough just to change the subject every time my mind drifts to something of real consequence. It's not enough to live only for the pursuit of pleasure as an end in itself. It's not enough to numb myself with choice distractions until it all comes to an abrupt ending. I thought it would be, and for a while it seemed like it was, but life on these terms is not enough.

The French philosopher and outspoken atheist Jean-Paul

Sartre once admitted, "That God does not exist, I cannot deny. That my whole being cries out for God, I cannot forget."[5]

More recently, another atheist author, Julian Barnes, wrote a memoir titled *Nothing to be Frightened Of*, documenting the thoughts and questions of an elderly man, preparing to face death, with no hope for or belief in anything but an abrupt ending to it all. He opened his memoir with this memorable sentence: "I don't believe in God, but I miss him."[6]

Part 2

THE STORY
OF JESUS

CHAPTER SIX

A WAY TO LIVE

Some may come to faith in God and to
love, without a conscious attachment to
Jesus. Both Nature and good men besides
Jesus may lead us to God. They who seek
God with all their hearts must, however,
some day on their way meet Jesus.

Heinrich Weinel, Jesus in the
Nineteenth Century and After

I've always admired anyone who attempts live comedy. It seems like one of the hardest, most potentially embarrassing ambitions imaginable. Of course, you have to be a funny person, but anyone can slip in a few witty comments over drinks with friends. Humor used while public speaking is a step closer, and a joke slipped unexpectedly into the lull of the keynote speech at a fundraising gala has a certain advantage. Laughter definitely comes easier when it sneaks up on an unsuspecting, probably bored audience. But standing in front of people who know your only goal is to make them laugh? That's another level. Everyone knows it's coming; they're watching your mechanics closely, listening for the buildup to the punch line. Live comedy is terrifying. And that's why I've always shown up and laughed—hard and loud—when a friend invites me to any sort of comedy gig.

It wasn't that difficult, because for years, I lived in the East

Village, where quite a few of my friends took improv comedy classes at Upright Citizens Brigade. The UCB theatre was just a few blocks from my apartment. When a friend would say, "My class is just wrapping up, and we're doing an improv show; please come to support!" I knew I could look super supportive with very little effort by taking a five-minute walk for a (free or at least very cheap) half-hour amateur improv show.

If you're totally unfamiliar with improv comedy, here are the basics: A scenario is given to a group of actors on the spot, and they act out the story as they go, entirely off-the-cuff. Usually, this leads to an enjoyable and ideally hilarious scene for everyone, but occasionally, the actors all have a different direction in mind and are struggling to follow each other's subtle cues. They somehow end up so far from the original premise that the story continues on but goes nowhere in particular. It's painful to watch.

That's when the class instructor has to get involved to salvage the story. The more unnoticeable, the better, but anyone paying attention can see it happen. The teacher casually inserts himself into the story, acts as one of the characters for a minute or two (however long it takes to get the story back on track, back to the parameters it was given to exist within from the start). As soon as the other actors have it, the very moment they've all remembered where this thing was going and started moving together in the right direction, the teacher exits stage right and lets the drama roll on.

This maneuver is called "recovering the plot," and that's exactly what the life of Jesus was all about.

The "plot" is most concisely understood in the four relationships that make up every human life: God, self, others, and the world. Regardless of age, gender, ethnicity, opportunity, historical era, or even belief, every person must fundamentally interact in these four spheres. This is the plot we are given, the plot we tend to drift from across the humdrum of so many ordinary Tuesdays, and the plot Jesus claimed he was recovering.

FOUR RELATIONSHIPS

God. We all must relate to God or our conception of God or our refusal to believe in a "god," but however you slice it, we all relate to some idea of the ultimate that is most commonly summed up in the word *God*.

Self. We are all cognizant of ourselves and therefore have a relationship with ourselves. We are self-aware and possess self-esteem. In fact, the person you think about most is almost certainly . . . yourself.

Others. We relate to other people. There's no escaping the ripple effects of other people's decisions—good and bad—that intersect with your life. Life is relationship to other people—the people you choose and the people you don't.

The World. We relate to the actual world we live in. We gather food from the earth, and the habits and decisions of our lives have large-scale consequences for the environment we inhabit.

The biblical story doesn't start with a messed-up world in need of fixing; it starts with a perfect world of pure relational bliss—unbroken, perfect relationship with God, with the self, with other people, and with the created world. All of this is summed up in the final words of Genesis 2: "Adam and his wife were both naked, and they felt no shame."

This is the description of this world as it was always meant to be, this life as it was meant to be lived. Doing and talking and listening before God without reservation, a sort of complete freedom before the divine that's nearly the opposite of what most people feel when walking through the doors of a church building.

But it gets better. There's freedom before one another too. Freedom to be themselves, to feel like themselves. And not in a defiant "I'll be me whether you like it or not" sort of way either. It was much more liberating than that. This was the purest form of relational freedom—really knowing yourself meant the freedom to truly see another person—selflessly loving others without the need to grit your teeth in determination.

The reason Adam and Eve were "naked and unashamed" is because shame had never entered human consciousness. No human being had ever been self-conscious. I mean that literally. No human being had ever thought primarily about himself or herself before, which is what you automatically do whenever you're exposed in any way.

When you are stripped of the way you'd like to present yourself, when you're "naked," you suddenly become conscious of yourself above all others. A teen is proven wrong in front of class and her intellect is exposed, so she instinctively runs inward, into herself. She becomes self-conscious, and from that self-centered place, she reacts, somehow providing for herself, protecting herself, or exalting herself. Sound familiar? That's the fate we're stuck with that is called sin. It happens with every sort of nakedness—physical, emotional, spiritual, and intellectual. We don't like to be exposed. We are guarded nearly all the time, but it wasn't always like this.

There was a time of only relational bliss. There was a place when people were seen all the way through and loved all the way through. There was a world where exposure wasn't feared; it just was. There was a relationship between God and people that didn't center on cause and effect or moral transaction or even parental give-and-take. It was delight. God and people enjoying one another's company with no strings attached, no unspoken demands, no passive-aggressive expectations. And it spilled over into a perfect view of the self, unconditional love for other people, and the sort of simple, ordinary harmony with creation we elusively call contentment.

Then mankind became conscious of the self and chose the self for the center, and the world you and I actually live in fell like a heavy velvet curtain at the end of the show. Only it wasn't the end of the show; it was the beginning. The Genesis summary of that sudden, fatal new normal reads like this:

> Then the eyes of both of them were opened, and they realized they were naked.
>
> *Genesis 3:7*

It's the antithesis of the perfection summarized only a few verses earlier. The darkness that covered the world when man chose himself for the center drove a chasm between every one of those four relationships—God, self, others, and the world.

God. Just like that, God seemed distant, unknowable, untrustable.

Self. Insecurity, shame, and self-consciousness plunged into the human heart for the first time. The emotions we spend our whole lives trying to escape were introduced into the story.

Others. In a moment, people went from "effortless love" to "effortless competition," fracturing into distinct groups, resorting even to violence because that's what self-provision, self-protection, and self-exaltation cost sometimes.

The World. And suddenly, a world in perfect cooperation is cursed with airborne disease and hard soil that requires harder work; a world bountifully working for its inhabitants began fighting against them.

Through one man, acting on behalf of us all, we lost the plot. We are still on the stage, still acting because the show must go on, but it's going on without a coherent story. We are still alive, but we've lost the way to truly live.

Through one man, acting on behalf of us all, we can recover the plot. We can remember the coherent story if the director will climb onto the stage as one of the actors and join in the drama. If he can recover the story, we can all pick it up again and remember our part. That's why the Bible calls Jesus "the last Adam."[1]

The story was far, far off course, so the director inserted himself into the story to recover the plot. By his life, we find a way to live.

CHAPTER SEVEN

GOD: THE SCANDAL OF *ABBA*

Then the man and his wife heard the
sound of the LORD God as he was walking
in the garden in the cool of the day, and
they hid from the LORD God among the
trees of the garden. But the LORD God
called to the man, "Where are you?"

He answered, "I heard you in the garden,
and I was afraid because I was naked;
so I hid."

Genesis 3:8–10

The first symptom of this "sin" thing is a warped view of God. Previously in Genesis, walking in the garden in the cool of the day is part of the normal routine for Adam and Eve. To them, God wasn't a riddle to be solved or an existential question. God was a Being to know and be known by, a Being as real as any of the creatures of his own creation, and a Being altogether good, sheltering them while also looking them in the eye and listening—the protection of a father and the intimacy of a friend. Then suddenly, God is feared, resisted, misunderstood, hidden from. That wasn't a momentary misconception; that was a new normal. It's all we've ever known.

In her book *Leaving Church*, Barbara Brown Taylor, herself a former Episcopalian priest with years of personal experience behind her thoughts, writes soberingly:

> One thing that had always troubled me was the way people disappeared from the church when their lives were breaking down. Separation and divorce were the most common explanations for long absences, but so were depression, alcoholism, job loss, and mortal illness. One new widow told me that she could not come to church because she started crying the moment she sat down in a pew. A young man freshly diagnosed with AIDS said that he stayed away because he was too frightened to answer questions and too angry to sing hymns. I understood their reasoning, but I was sorry that church did not strike these wounded souls as a place they could bring the dark fruits of their equally dark nights.[1]

Sadly, I have watched a similar pattern as a pastor. It's a theme that can be traced all the way back to the very beginning:

> Then the man and his wife heard the sound of the LORD God as he was walking in the garden in the cool of the day, and they hid from the LORD God among the trees of the garden.
>
> *Genesis 3:8*

There was a time when God could be trusted, when the Creator was Father, Mother, Protector, Comforter, and Friend. But to our ears, that sounds like a fairy tale. A long, long time ago, that image of God got traded in for the God you're more familiar with—distant, unknowable, untrustable. A God whose company many welcome in their best moments, but equally a God we instinctively keep a distance from in our worst.

ABBA

Jesus of Nazareth. He was a Jewish peasant from a rural family in a nothing town occupied by Roman soldiers who had long ago proved their domination and were just waiting for a reason to refresh everyone's memory. He showed up at the temple, the one place the Romans didn't touch, the one place the Jewish people could ask for help from a God who, although he seemed distant most of the time, had supposedly come through on a national scale in past dire circumstances. So the Pharisees, the priests of Jesus' day, added rules to an absurdly long list of rules—613 to be exact. Their plan was simple. Maybe we can live holy enough lives to get God's attention again, because the God of our ancestors seems to be apathetic or uncaring or distracted or some combination of the three. Maybe we can follow his rules precisely enough to convince him to stretch out that strong right hand we've heard so much about. Jesus shows up to their temple and starts praying.

When Jesus prayed, he called God "Abba," and that was a showstopper. It was scandalous. It was the sort of thing that didn't belong anywhere in the temple, much less out of the mouth of a rabbi. You see, Israel already knew God's name—it was Yahweh. That's how it looks in English, at least. In Hebrew, a written language made up of only consonants, it's YHWH. The way they arrived at that name shows the incomparable reverence they had for God.

When God identified himself to Abraham (the man whom Christianity, Judaism, and Islam all trace their roots back to), he said, "I am El-Shaddai."[2] In a Canaanite world that believed in many gods over many nations, El meant "king of the gods." El-Shaddai was the Canaanite way of saying, "I'm the king of all the gods, but I'm also so much more than what you conceive of when you hear that name."

Later, God introduces himself to Moses (the guy who led Israel out of Egyptian slavery). In that famous burning-bush moment that changed Moses from a meek shepherd to a meek abolitionist, God called himself, "I AM WHO I AM," meaning, "I am the unchanging one, the one who has always been, the one who will always be." Through a bunch of ancient language technicalities you'll thank me not to go into detail about, *YHWH* is Hebrew shorthand for "I AM WHO I AM." It's a way of saying God is incomprehensibly constant. He is completely "other" from our humanness in all the best ways.[3]

Still, over time, for the serious Jew, even that name wasn't reverent enough. After all, the Ten Commandments do include, "Thou shalt not take the name of the LORD [*YHWH*] thy God in vain." If Old English is confusing, an updated translation reads, "You shall not misuse the name of the LORD [*YHWH*] your God."[4] Attempting to be sure God's people didn't even get close to violating that command, they stopped calling God by his own name altogether, replacing his name with titles like *Adonai*, meaning, "Lord." It's the ancient equivalent of calling someone "sir." Respectful, formal, and keeping the proper distance.

All that reverence, multiplied over many generations and hundreds of years, and then Jesus walked into their temple and called God *Abba*. But why is using a different name so scandalous?

The New Testament was written in ancient Greek, but *Abba* is an Aramaic term. The elite spoke Greek. The educated spoke Greek. Books were written in Greek. History was recorded in Greek, the language of the distinguished. Aramaic was the language that still stuck to Israel from seventy years exiled in Babylon, their previous conqueror. It was the language of the common peasants, the blue-collar, minimum-wage day laborers. It was also the language of Jesus, according to the majority of first-century scholarship.

The earliest manuscripts of the Gospels—Matthew, Mark, Luke, and John, the four biographical accounts of Jesus' life—are written in Greek, with only a few exceptions, including *Abba*, the name Jesus gave God. *Abba* went untranslated because there is no direct translation. There is no equivalent Greek term. In Aramaic, *Abba* was the most intimate term one could possibly call a father. The closest thing we have in English is a toddler using the name "Dada," but that doesn't quite do it because *Abba* wasn't a cheesy name you used as a kid and then grew out of with age. It wasn't a name you'd be embarrassed to be caught saying to your father as a twentysomething. It was a term of endearment from a son to a father that was lost in translation because it was so rarely used, or maybe so rarely needed. The Greeks didn't have a term like *Abba* because no one would address their father with that much intimacy. Jesus spoke to Yahweh with such familiarity we can't even translate it.

German theologian Joachim Jeremias writes, "There is not a single example of the use of *Abba* . . . as an address to God in the whole of Jewish literature."[5] A new way of praying was born. No one else talked to God like that because that's not how you speak to an authority whose name you can't stomach saying out loud and whose favor you're trying to coax through moral perfection. So where did Jesus get the idea he could talk to God like a kid whose dad had just come back from a business trip with souvenirs and presents? From God himself.

Most people think Jesus lived his whole life leading an uprising through very compelling teaching and the rumor of miraculous powers, but it didn't actually play out like that. Until he reached the age of thirty, Jesus' life was ordinary enough that historians considered next to none of it worth writing down. His ministry lasted approximately thirty-six months, from age thirty to thirty-three. So if you take his claims at face value, the vast majority of the life of the divine-human was pretty forgettable. What happened at age thirty to turn the tide?

BAPTISM

The event that kick-started a three-year revolution the world still hasn't recovered from is Jesus' baptism, when he was submerged in the Jordan River by a radical country preacher. Plenty of people got baptized by John in the Jordan. Crowds were flocking to him. That's why there happened to be plenty of witnesses at this bend in the river on the day Jesus turned up. Tons of people trekked there every day, so some peasant from Nazareth asking for baptism was like grabbing a number at a deli and waiting to be called, but when the Nazarene's number was called, it got interesting—very interesting. The sky parted, a dove descended,[6] and an audible voice was heard declaring, "This is my Son, whom I love; with him I am well pleased."[7]

The order of events is important. God claims Jesus as his own, declares his love, and speaks pleasure over him before Jesus utters a single word of teaching, works a miracle, or does anything publicly that anyone else thought worth remembering. God made the first move.

Jesus called God "*Abba*" because God had made it clear that's exactly who he is.

And when Jesus prays, when he talks to God, a certain homesickness arises in me. I want what he has. I miss it like someone who has had it before, maybe only for a moment, and I forget what it feels like most of the time, but when I slow down long enough to actually consider Jesus, there's a vague familiarity that gives way to longing. He actually believed what God said.

WHO IS GOD?

Who do you believe God is? The looming darkness that both you and I live under convinces us that God is someone other than who he has always been and who Jesus confirmed he still is. The first effect of sin is to hide from the God who is just looking to take an afternoon stroll in the shade like he's suddenly going to turn on us when he sees who we really are.

A. W. Tozer famously said, "What comes into our minds when we think about God is the most important thing about us."[8]

Stop reading for a moment and picture God (or your Higher Power or Universal Truth or Love Personified—whatever title you prefer). Picture God. What is God like? If you've never thought long and hard about that question, you should. Because whether you realize it or not, you will always live in response to your answer to that question.

If your image of God is that he is a stern, harsh rule maker, then you will live like you're always being graded, constantly being watched and evaluated. You'll believe the truest thing about you is the final mark you receive as the sum total of your days.

If your image of God is a permissive, laid-back dad with a headful of curls, making you an omelet in a tie-dye T-shirt, then you will live like your actions in this world are not of ultimate value, that at the end of the day, what you do does not matter in any significant way. When it comes to mistakes, this can be relieving, but what about when it comes to virtue? If your actions are insignificant in the fall of this world, they are also insignificant in the redemption of it.

If your image of God is an all-powerful Being far too busy with far too many things to be interested in your one ordinary life, then you will live like you are of little importance. You will have a humble awareness of your small-ness, but no loving awareness of your value.

If your image of God is a divine watchmaker who set the universe in place and has moved on to other projects and all but forgotten about this one, you will live like this life and this world are forgettable, like you and those around you are forgettable. You will believe that this world is not the stage of the grand story but nothing more than a sideshow amidst a sea of sideshows.

If your view of God is a beautiful accident of scientific factors that led to an explosion of matter, then you will be forced to live like what you do, the effect it has on others, and who you become is nothing more than accidental. You are forced to believe that what you do and who you are does not matter, at least not in any ultimate sense.

So that brings us back to Tozer's famous question, the one he calls the most important question: "Who or what comes to your mind when you think about God?"

Rabbi Abraham Joshua Heschel wrote, "Prayer is our humble answer to the inconceivable surprise of living."[9] We all wake up to a mystery, even if it's just the mystery of our own lives. I know nothing about you, and you know nothing about me—apart from what's offered you in these pages. Still, there is something quite significant we know about each other. You and I both woke up this morning to a day we must somehow live, to a self we must somehow be, and to a mystery we will never completely figure out, never reach the end of.[10] Prayer, in the broadest sense, is how we live out our ordinary days in the presence of that mystery. It is the outward expression of what comes to our minds when we think about God.

Jesus' prayers showed us who he really believed God to be— *Abba*. Your prayers do the same. It doesn't matter if your prayers come out in communal liturgy, read aloud together in a sacred building or in the back of your head, never audible, and only after you've exhausted every other option. If you want to know what you really think of God, just pay attention to your prayers.

Perhaps Nancy Mairs said it best, or at least most directly: "Who one believes God to be is most accurately revealed not in any credo but in the way one speaks to God when no one else is listening."[11]

So here's what Jesus' prayers tell us he believes about God: "I am his Son, whom he loves; with me he is well pleased."

We are wandering around the stage, not recognizing the voice of the director anymore, so God inserted himself into the story and recovered the plot. That's what Jesus' prayers and baptism were all about.

CHAPTER EIGHT

SELF: THE TROUBLE WITH FIG LEAVES

Then the eyes of both of them were
opened, and they realized they were
naked; so they sewed fig leaves together
and made coverings for themselves.
Genesis 3:7

I awkwardly walked into a sterile conference room at a corporate retreat center outside of Chicago on a Sunday evening in July. It was the first retreat of a three-year program I had impulsively signed up for at a friend's recommendation and then more or less forgotten about until today. And here I was, one of approximately two hundred Christian leaders arriving for an intensive spiritual formation retreat.

We were all strangers to each other. We had flown in from every corner of North America, sharing nothing but a broad vocation. We received a quick welcome before heading to dinner, where I'd stand awkwardly holding a lunch tray and scanning for an empty seat among the sea of tables for the first time since I was fourteen.

At the welcome, the conference hosts did what they could to break the ice and then gave us a single rule for that first meal: You can't tell anyone else what you do. Go ahead and share your name, share where you're from, share about your family. But "I pastor this church or run this nonprofit" is strictly off-limits.

The logic was simple. We are all addicted to relating to people through a role. For years we've been identifying ourselves by a particular function in the lives of others. "So here you'll learn again to just be souls on a journey. That's who you really are anyway." Admittedly, it was strange sitting at dinner that first night when we all arrived. Two hundred strangers trying to carry on conversations with one another without explaining ourselves the way we'd all become accustomed to explaining ourselves.

I shared a table with Sue and Phil. I knew there was a whole role they filled—a way they were used to being known, a way everyone else knew them—but to this day, I just know Sue and Phil. I know where they came from, who's important to them, what they like, and how they rest.

And I was just "Tyler," without all the dressing up I've done my best to add on to that name. I was known the way everybody knew me when I was a kid, before I discovered I could pick and choose from a catalog of ways to decorate that given name. I was just Tyler. There was something humanizing about that.

The surprising claim on the Bible's opening page is that in the beginning, before you did a single thing—before you succeeded or failed, before you became something or nothing, before you proved them wrong or right, before you stood up on your own two shaky feet or crumbled in shame—in the beginning, there was God, nothing but the Spirit of God hovering over the surface of the deep, with you on his mind.

Eugene Peterson sums up the Genesis claim as "my identity does not begin when I begin to understand myself. There is something previous to what I think about myself, and it is what God thinks of me. That means that everything I think and feel is by nature a response, and the one to whom I respond is God. I never speak the first word. I never make the first move."[1]

As we get older, our identity is supposed to expand. We are supposed to grow into our given names, to become more full, more alive, more whole. Our identity was made to grow and grow, but instead the opposite almost always happens—our identity shrinks. As we get older, our dreams get smaller. Our eyes go from wide and full of wonder to narrow, with our heads down on today's agenda. Who I believe I am and who I believe everyone else is become narrower—at least in part because rather than living into the name we are given, we exchange it.

Professor.

Actor.

Entrepreneur.

Mother.

Filmmaker.

Convict.

Pastor.

The Genesis story calls this disastrous exchange "fig leaves":

> Then the eyes of both of them were opened, and they realized they were naked; so they sewed fig leaves together and made coverings for themselves.
>
> *Genesis 3:7*

They realized they were naked. They became self-conscious. For the first time, human beings turned their focus inward and felt the need to cover up, to hide parts of themselves while intentionally presenting others, to put on a best self, a public self.

Fig leaves—it was the world's first attempt to control self-perception. Since that day, we've never managed to stop feeling the need to do the same. Adam and Eve reached for fig leaves, and the whole world became a fashion show.

After God publicly called Jesus "Son," Jesus paraded around calling everyone within earshot brother and sister.[2] In effect,

Jesus was saying, "Everyone who wants God's fathering, gets it. We are all God's children." Sweet sentiment, right? Actually it's much more than sentiment. There's much more concrete reality to this claim than we give it credit for.

Today, a family name doesn't matter much outside of where you're alphabetized in a stack of other random names, but in the ancient world, a family name was everything. Before individualism took over, the family name dictated status, opportunity, and image. Not just anyone could pull himself up by his bootstraps and make something of his life. The class you were born into, summed up in a surname—the part parents didn't get to pick—was the most defining thing about you. It was your unshakable status.

The implications, obviously, are that certain opportunities and pursuits are restricted by name. Regardless of intellect or skill, name bracketed your employment opportunities, standard of living, and social circles. Then, of course, there's the perception problem. Your last name told a long, long story about you that you didn't write. So much was assumed about you by everyone else, based on your name.

At this point, you may be tempted to think we've made a lot of progress since those archaic days, but before you assume we've arrived at a societal utopia free of past ills, grading one another on a totally just scale, an equally honest diagnosis of our own society is advised. Modern society hasn't removed things like status, opportunity, and image; it just made adjustments to their source.

My last name is Staton. No one cares. No one has ever in my life commented on my name unless they were asking how to spell it or pronounce it. Here's what people want to know about—my résumé. Here's where my status, opportunity, and image come from—my résumé. If you're a business executive, it may mean a résumé in the most traditional sense (a document listing your educational and employment history), but if you're a freelance designer or a stay-at-home mom or an aspiring artist, the résumé is an abstract version of exactly the same thing—like a social media profile or just the "self" you put on when you bump into an acquaintance at the grocery store.

In the ancient world, a family name was kept squeaky-clean for the sake of controlling, or at least trying to control, perception. Your family name was a mirror, revealing who you really were. It was guarded at all cost because it followed you around everywhere you went. Your name defined who you were when you walked into a room, what you could and could not do in this life, and your inherent worth in the world. No one was completely honest about their family name. There was too much at stake.

In the modern world, a résumé functions exactly the same way. We do our best to keep it squeaky-clean in an attempt to control perception. Because, at the end of the day, what is a résumé anyway? It's your preferred perception. No one has ever been completely honest on a résumé. No one has ever handed an interviewer a document that read, "I'll be super motivated and attentive for a couple weeks, and then I'll settle into the real me. My personal email will always sit open alongside my work email, causing me to frequently spend upward of fifteen minutes searching for the perfect GIF to reply to a thread about Saturday plans with friends. I'll find a way to stretch my lunch hour and routinely ease back into work by scrolling on Facebook to take inventory of the chronically frustrating political comments of distant relatives. Eventually, most of my creative energy will be dedicated to passively-aggressively trying to figure out how early I can leave in the evening without jeopardizing my upward mobility."

Résumés aren't honest; they're ideal. And that's because there's too much at stake. Your résumé hangs over you, telling you how much you matter in a particular room, what you can and cannot do in this life, and your inherent worth in this world. The modern West has guarded the free expression of the individual more than ever before, and much of that is very, very good. But a by-product is that we live with an inescapable need to prove ourselves. The side effect of a society where you get to invent your own self-worth is a dearth of intimacy. Everyone else becomes a scale I must be weighed on. Everyone else becomes a mirror who must tell me who I am. Everyone else is a person I'm competing against or a vote of approval I'm competing for. These side effects make intimacy impossible.

Family means intimacy. It means people who couldn't care less about how big of a deal you become or don't become because they'll never care too much for your résumé anyway. Family means people who you're supposed to be able to rest in the company of, savor the intimacy of being known more completely than anywhere else, and enjoy the truest kind of friendship that sees another for their unique BE-ing, not their ability to produce by DO-ing.

In a world where people define themselves and others by surname, in a world where people are defined by résumé, Jesus tells an alternative story.

THE PRODIGAL GOD

Jesus' teaching method was mostly to tell one story after another, substituting different characters, hoping that maybe this version of the same story would catch someone for whom the other parallels didn't do it. Jesus' most famous story is commonly known as "The Prodigal Son."[3] Charles Dickens, who knew a thing or two about storytelling, is widely rumored to have called it the greatest story ever told.[4] It went something like this:

There were these two brothers.

The older one lived by the book. You know the type. He was a people pleaser. He thought mathematically—very right-brained—and he had a plan: work his way up the ladder, one step at a time, eyes permanently fixed on the ultimate goal, the assumed ending, which was to take over the family business. It was all very sensible and predictable.

The younger one was all free spirit and come what may. People said he was reacting against his goody-two-shoes older brother, defining himself by not being him, but his dad knew better. He saw something different in him from the get-go. The firstborn ate and slept and pooped like clockwork, but this newborn? It seemed like he'd never sleep. His eyes darted around every room. He was awake all night, every night (seemed like it anyway). He was anything but predictable.

The older brother was judicious. He appreciated growing up in a nice home, with three square meals a day, a business his father worked into a conglomerate, and a future that was more or less set up. The younger brother resented all of it. The employees whispered that he was spoiled, but his dad always thought of it as the best kind of restlessness—that combination of curiosity and adventure. Everyone except his father was surprised when he announced at his own graduation party, "Look, Pops, this has never been me. Why wait my whole life (or, more accurately, *your* whole life) for me to collect my share and go my own way?" If the staff and family were surprised at the request, their jaws really hit the floor when it was granted.

So he was gone. A well-off eighteen-year-old with a wide-eyed, if not naive, view of the world and a pretty big financial safety net to catch him if he fell. And he fell like an amateur trapeze artist wearing a weight vest.

He fancied himself a starving artist on the run, which is always easier to do when you can outfit the "artist vibe" with designer clothes and a bar tab deep enough to make plenty of friends. Maybe he was an artist, but he definitely wasn't starving. It didn't take long until he was living in a wide-open loft with plenty of exposed brick, a 24/7 doorman, and a rooftop hot tub overlooking the Mediterranean. What seemed like a blessing turned out to be a curse.

Three years later, he was the oldest twenty-one you can imagine—multiple stints in rehab, an alcohol problem he didn't have the energy to address right now, a son of his own he was too ashamed to meet, and a rap sheet that included a couple of brief stints in prison for soliciting prostitution. He was informed that his account balance had finally bottomed out when he was getting a money order at a sketchy Western Union conveniently located just outside the holding cells.

He got his first real job out of pure desperation. He left the city unannounced after spending the full inheritance. He couldn't face those friends, that landlord, that young boy of his, without the money that had made him. There was a pork slaughterhouse just beyond the city limits. He was the first, and only, Jew they had ever had on staff. Kosher diets and bacon factories don't mix. Payday seemed doable when he got hired on Tuesday. He could wait until Friday to eat. But by midafternoon on Wednesday, he was already broken. His supervisor caught him face-first in the same pile of wet mush they use to fatten up the swine, and that was grounds for immediate termination.

Hitchhiking back to Dad's place was rock-bottom. He smoked a full pack of Reds pacing back and forth at the end of the long driveway, planning his speech, exactly how he'd lay it out: "Sir, I know I'm not your son anymore. I threw that away a long time ago. Would you consider me for a job? I'm prepared to work my way up. I'll sleep in the barn with the servants who keep the livestock, and minimum wage is more than enough for me, if you happen to have an open position, and if there isn't a more qualified application already in hand, would you consider me . . . sir?"

He didn't get the job. He didn't get a bunk in the servants' quarters. He got much, much more than that.

The first step down the driveway was the hardest one to take, but he didn't take many after that. He heard the commotion first and then looked up from his feet to see his dad hiking up his royal purple robes and coming in a full-out sprint his way. He basically tackled him, cracking up while a couple of tears ran down his cheeks. He kissed him right on the mouth, Marlboro breath and all.

The unexpected welcome threw him off for a moment, but he pushed his father back and started into the speech. "Sir, I know I'm not—" That was all he got out. He was interrupted by the orders fired off: "Get all the bottles of that vintage cab the Mrs. likes so much out of the wine cellar. Haven't we been dry aging some beef? Tonight's the night! Hire the band from last New Year's Eve and invite everyone!" Turning back toward his ragged, bony youngest, he spoke so fast and with so much excitement that he could hardly get it out: "Every morning and every night for three years, I've been up before the sun, staring out the window at the end of the driveway, hoping to see you. My boy's home! My son! My son is back!" Turning back toward the staff, he instructed, "Oh, and before I forget, have him sign the revised will." As it turned out, the very moment the boy had walked off the property, his father had redone the family will, cutting him back in. Even when he thought he was broke, his account balance was full, awaiting his signature. There was not a single moment in his life when he was truly on his own.

The wine was flowing, the steak was medium rare, the band was loud, and a surprise firework display lit up the night. The older brother sat furiously in his office, crunching the numbers on the cost of the impromptu party. It wasn't fiscally responsible. It wasn't fair. How do you throw away a couple of decades' worth of profits and stroll back in like nothing happened? His dad poked his head in the office for just a second: "Son, come down. I poured you a glass and requested your favorite song. I can't party without my firstborn!" Annoyed, the son's eyes just turned back to his spreadsheet.

Neither the "do all the right things with an assumed reward" older brother nor the "chain-smoking, daydreaming, painfully insecure" younger brother get what they think they deserve in the end. Neither of them understand how generous their father really is.

For centuries, this story has been commonly called "The Prodigal Son," and it's known on some level by almost everyone, regardless of whether they believe it's from the mouth of God or from the imagination of a very gifted (but very human) teacher, or if it was dreamed up by a complete quack. Despite its notoriety, I've never heard the word *prodigal* used, except in reference to this story. It's just not common in normal conversation. *Prodigal* is defined as "spending money or resources freely and recklessly; wastefully extravagant; having or giving something on a lavish scale." Basically, *prodigal* means "recklessly generous." It means "giving and giving and giving, to a degree most people would call a waste." It's for this very reason that author and theologian Tim Keller calls this story "the Prodigal God."[5] It's not the younger brother who's reckless; the father, representing God, is the reckless one.

Ancient Israel was an honor-shame culture. The picture Jesus painted through this story was actually a familiar, relatively common picture in the culture to which he was speaking. Everyone in that original crowd thought they knew where the story was going. The meeting between the father and son mirrors a *kezazah* ceremony. Among first-century Jews, if a son humiliated his father by rejecting him, bringing shame not only on him but on the entire family name and then had the audacity to show his face in the wider community again, he was greeted by a village-wide ceremony.

The entire community gathered on the border of the village, while the rebellious son stood opposite them. Then one representative would step forward, smash a clay pot on the ground, and let out a full-throated scream, "You are now cut off from your people!" The clay pot represented the community's view of the rebellious individual—totally broken, irredeemable, no longer useful for any purpose. The English word *ostracize*, meaning "to exile or banish from a people or community," is derived from the ancient Greek term *ostrakizo*, meaning "to banish by the vote of the people written on a potsherd." The modern concept of being ostracized is derived from the Hebrew *kezazah* ceremony.

When the father ran out to greet the son—family members, friends, day laborers from the community all gathering around—the original listeners would've been thinking, *Here it comes. The breaking of the clay pot. Finally the father can distance himself from his son's embarrassing behavior. Finally the father can stop wearing the shame of his offspring. Finally he can get a bit of closure on this parental nightmare.* Then it happens. He wraps his arm around his son. He slips a signet ring onto his finger, symbolizing rule and authority over the estate. He wraps a robe around his shoulders, the sort of robe worn by the ruler of the house. He wasn't interested in undressing himself of his son's shame. The father was prepared to wear that shame to the grave. He was interested in clothing his son with the honor that this younger son, not realizing it until it was much too late, had undressed himself of when he walked off the property with a check to cash. This was the twist ending.

Jesus told this story to a crowd of people familiar with loyal sons who took up the family business and rebellious sons who ran off and threw it all away, but this image of the father would have been completely foreign. The father was the reckless one. The father was the prodigal. Jesus is doing his best to make sure we know we are not dealing with an authoritative overseer or a micromanaging boss or even a well-intentioned and hurt father of a disappointing, wayward child; we are dealing with a prodigal God.

Jesus was a small-town rabbi with only a few followers selected from the already picked over group of leftovers after all the other rabbis were done. He walked into the temple, and everyone expected him to follow the rules. But he didn't. He lived like there's a prodigal God on the other side of the cosmos—a God so generous that *wasteful* is the most appropriate word; a God so loving that he paces in front of the window daily, hoping that today might be the day you come dragging your feet stubbornly down the dirt road; a God so good that he will sit down and rehash everything that happened while you were gone if you want, but if you're into it, he's hoping to uncork a rare vintage from the wine cellar and invite all your friends over for filet mignon and dancing. It's all the same to him, so whichever you prefer.

A RECURRING DREAM

I only have anecdotal evidence to support this, but it seems like the most common nightmare is a comical one: you show up somewhere ordinary but public and begin going about an everyday activity, and then, like a freight train, it hits you— you're naked.

For me, it's my elementary school cafeteria. Why? I have no idea, but I could describe exactly what that lunchroom looked like, right down to the minor details, because I've seen it over and over in my dreams. I'm sitting down with a slice of rectangular pizza and a chocolate milk, and the plastic stool seat feels cold against my bare cheeks. I'm naked! Everyone else has known for a while, and it's just hitting me.

Maybe we all have that dream a few times in our lives, because it's connected to something true somewhere deep in our history. The first nightmare was about nakedness, and we've never woken up from it.

Fig leaves come in the form of skimpy outfits on the curbside, Armani suits and 24-karat cuff links, clerical collars, and everything in between. All of these are coverings, and all are covering the same things—insecurity, shame, and self-consciousness.

The open secret of ancient Israel and of the modern West is that "making it" and getting whatever comes along with your version of success don't actually cure insecurity, erase shame, or still the constant churn of restlessness that drove you along the journey toward success. The subtext of Jesus' masterful "Prodigal God" parable is that both sons are trying to "make it." One thinks success is staying home, the other adventure, and both fail.

WHO ARE YOU?

Who are you? What position or perception do you use to define yourself? What do you have that, if you lost it, you wouldn't know who you are anymore?

A. W. Tozer claimed that nothing exceeds the importance of our view of God.[6] The literary giant C. S. Lewis doesn't argue with the importance of one's conception of the divine, though he does believe it holds second place (at best) in a list of defining ideas: "I read in a periodical the other day that the fundamental thing is how we think of God. By God Himself, it is not! How God thinks of us is not only more important, but infinitely more important. Indeed how we think of Him is of no importance except insofar as it is related to how He thinks of us."[7]

Some of the father's final words in Jesus' "Prodigal God" story—words addressed to the older son but applicable to the younger son as well—are telling:

> "You are always with me, and everything I have is yours."
>
> *Luke 15:31*

God does not treat us as we deserve. He does not repay us according to our actions. He does not sit behind a desk, flipping through a stack of résumés. He assures us that no amount of wandering will change who we are. He assures us that no past offense, no mismanagement of his resources, will cause him to become stingy. Squander half the estate, and he just cuts us right back into the will. Frederick Buechner writes:

> What Genesis suggests is that this original self, with the print of God's thumb still upon it, is the most essential part of who we are and is buried deep in all of us as a source of wisdom and strength and healing which we can draw upon or, with our terrible freedom, not draw upon as we choose . . . The original, shimmering self gets buried so deep that most of us end up hardly living out of it at all. Instead we live out all the other selves which we are constantly putting on and taking off like coats and hats against the world's weather.[8]

Whatever form it takes, human history is a fashion show—a bunch of attempts to control perception through wearing the most appropriate fig leaves. Jesus' life wasn't about better coverings; it was about shameless nakedness.

We forgot who we were, so he recovered the plot.

It's that profoundly simple prayer of Søren Kierkegaard: "Now with God's help I shall become myself."[9]

It's what Mary Karr describes near the end of her trilogy of memoirs: "It feels as if I was made—from all the possible shapes a human might take—not to prove myself worthy but to refine the worth I'm formed from, acknowledge it, own it, spend it on others."[10]

Spend it on others. Jesus recovered that part of the plot too.

CHAPTER NINE

OTHERS: LEPERS, PROSTITUTES, AND TAX COLLECTORS

"The woman you put here with me—she gave me some fruit from the tree, and I ate it."
Genesis 3:12

There's a scene near the beginning of *The Brothers Karamazov* when person after person is making the trip to the local monastery for a word with the all-wise elder. It's a fascinating flurry of sage wisdom. There's one seeker, in particular, who has always gotten my attention.

An old man, a physician, unquestionably intelligent, describes his query. "'I love mankind,' he said, 'but I am amazed at myself: the more I love mankind in general, the less I love people in particular, that is, individually, as separate persons.'" He goes on.

> "And yet I am incapable of living in the same room with anyone for even two days, this I know from experience. As soon as someone is there, close to me, his personality oppresses my self-esteem and restricts my freedom. In twenty-four hours I can begin to hate even the best of men: one because he takes too long eating his dinner, another because he has a cold and keeps blowing his nose. I become the enemy of people the

moment they touch me . . . On the other hand, it has always happened that the more I hate people individually, the more ardent becomes my love for humanity as a whole."[1]

He's noticing a gap between his intention and his action that he can't seem to close, a troubling space between his philosophy of people and his actual interpersonal relationships with those very people.

The elder responds insightfully, "Active love is a harsh and fearful thing compared with love in dreams."[2]

The idea of love in my imagination is much better than my actual attempts to love an individual person. Wouldn't you agree? Our capacity for love, in general, and struggle to love, in particular, is a disturbing diagnosis.

The trouble with sin isn't that God has a tight moral grid—and coloring within the lines is how we prove we're on his side. It's that sin inhibits us from doing what we were made to do—love. To minor on sin is to minor on love because sin constricts the capacity for love. Sin is a big issue to God because love is a big issue to God. If I pretend sin is a minor issue for me, I unintentionally make love a minor issue for me too.

"The woman you put here with me—she gave me some fruit from the tree, and I ate it."[3] These are the first words Adam speaks to God when he comes out of hiding in a killer pair of green, leafy shorts. It didn't take long for self-consciousness to turn into blame. A rock fell into a lake without banks, and the ripples in the water hit the self first, but they quickly moved out from there to touch every relationship the self touches. In a single moment, disunity, distrust, accusation, competition, jealousy, loneliness, and the like came to stay. The idea of "the other" is invented in reaction to self-consciousness.

The Author wrote himself into his own story that had wandered so far he could barely recognize it. Jesus felt the ripple effects that went out from those first words of blame. He was born into the peasant class of an oppressed people group and forced to live as a refugee until the age of twelve, and it didn't get a whole lot better after that.

In the Ancient Near Eastern world Jesus grew up in, Jews lived separate from Romans and Greeks. From the Jewish perspective, there were Gentile people, whose culture was commonly thought of as a corrupting poison to be feared, so the Jewish people hid themselves away from the Gentile cities across the Sea of Galilee. Then there were Samaritans, those who had a different twist on interpretation of the Hebrew Torah. They weren't so much feared as looked down on, thought of as less than; they'd be pitied if they weren't so detestable.

And within the Jewish community itself, there were class lines. Priests and peasants and everyone else found their slot somewhere in the middle. There were strong convictions on the same sacred literature expressed through various sects— Pharisees, Sadducees, Zealots, and Essenes. The fractures in society could be seen from far away, massive cracks running between groups of people, but zoom in and you'd just find more of the same—tiny cracks splintering even groups of people who seemed to share so much. The fear of, accusation toward, and competition with "the other," whomever that other may be, knew no bounds.

That shouldn't be too difficult to imagine. Look around the world today and take in the consequences of self-consciousness rippling through the waters for a couple of thousand more years since then.

PROSTITUTES, LEPERS, AND TAX COLLECTORS

In New York, being a pastor doesn't win me any popularity contests. Usually, when I'm getting to know someone, I dread the "what do you do?" question I know is coming because I know the disappointed "Really? You seemed so normal," look that always follows my answer.

In Jesus' hometown, though, being a part of the priesthood was socially as good as it gets—a status symbol for a first-century Jew. The Pharisees, the elite group of priests who more or less controlled the temple (and therefore the Jewish population) were the most powerful and prestigious members of their society.

If you trace that same social and moral hierarchy all the way to the bottom, you'll find three groups occupying the basement—prostitutes, lepers, and tax collectors. In fact, it is widely suspected that those three groups had managed to get themselves categorically expelled from the temple, not even allowed to cross the threshold, lest they contaminate the holy building with their filthy presence. According to the Talmud, which details the ceremonial laws that governed ancient Judaism, cleansing rituals made it next to impossible for a prostitute to achieve temple access. A tax collector could technically participate but many believe the priests of the first century wouldn't have allowed it, and even a healed leper who followed the very strict laws of purification[4] after healing would be relegated to the "Chamber of Lepers," a separate seating section for those lucky enough to inexplicably recover from the disease.

Prostitutes

No self-respecting priest would be caught sharing the company of a prostitute. Can you imagine the perception problem? These were serious men with a reputation to protect.

A particularly curious Pharisee once invited Jesus over for dinner. Never one to turn down a well-seasoned lamb shank, Jesus showed up. Somewhere between dinner and dessert, a prostitute barged into the dining room, unannounced and certainly uninvited.

The loud makeup, scant clothing, and used body matched

the street corner she occupied, but here in the home of a priest, she didn't match the backdrop. Every guest at the table looked her up and down, taking in the spectacle—everyone except Jesus. He was looking her straight in the eye. That's when she recognized him. She had heard the rumors. She was even at the back of the crowd when he taught once. She managed to walk away with a rehearsed cool and withdrawn aura about her, but it took a bit more effort than usual. She couldn't stop thinking about what he said. It was haunting her in the best way.

Before the host could object, she had wedged herself between Jesus and his place setting. On her knees, she wept while pouring out a jar of perfume on his feet. The smell filled the room, covering up the scent of roasted figs and honey coming out from the kitchen. This was the good stuff, top shelf. God only knows how many tricks she had turned to finance that bottle. She washed his feet with the perfume and dried them with the only rag available—her own hair.

The priest hosting the dinner, first outraged by the intrusion, had settled into a smug sense of pride. *Prophet?* he thought. *This guy's a fraud. If he knew the mind of God, he'd know exactly who this woman is and exactly what God thinks of her. There's no way he'd put up with this.*

Jesus interrupts his train of thought, speaking abruptly to this priest, Simon by name:

Jesus answered him, "Simon, I have something to tell you."

"Tell me, teacher," he said.

"Two people owed money to a certain moneylender. One owed him five hundred denarii, and the other fifty. Neither of them had the money to pay him back, so he forgave the debts of both. Now which of them will love him more?"

Simon replied, "I suppose the one who had the bigger debt forgiven."

"You have judged correctly," Jesus said.

Then he turned toward the woman and said to Simon, "Do you see this woman? I came into your house. You did not give me any water for my feet, but she wet my feet with her tears and wiped them with her hair. You did not give me a kiss, but this woman, from the time I entered, has not stopped kissing my feet. You did not put oil on my head, but she has poured perfume on my feet. Therefore, I tell you, her many sins have been forgiven—as her great love has shown. But whoever has been forgiven little loves little."

Then Jesus said to her, "Your sins are forgiven."

The other guests began to say among themselves, "Who is this who even forgives sins?"

Jesus said to the woman, "Your faith has saved you; go in peace."

Luke 7:40–50

As it turned out, Jesus did know exactly who she was and exactly what God thought of her. She was a beloved daughter of the Father. It wasn't God who had drawn dividing lines between people; the priests did that all on their own.

For the sexually shamed, economically trapped, and religiously shunned, Jesus told a better story. He recovered the plot.

Lepers

Immediately following his most famous sermon, Jesus walked out from behind the podium (or, in this case, off a mountainside) and was greeted by a man with leprosy who fell at Jesus' knees and said in desperation, "Lord, if you are willing, you can make me clean."[5]

Receiving a confirmed diagnosis of a highly contagious, incurable disease has to be debilitating. I can't imagine what it's like to walk out of a doctor's office with the weight of that sort of news, but the problem was multiplied for lepers. They wore their disease on their skin. There was no hiding the diagnosis. It would consume them for the rest of their lives. Moving from barely noticeable to difficult to conceal to the first and only thing anyone saw when they looked at you. Leper—that's who they are now. That's all anyone will see.

Leprosy was feared for all the obvious reasons, but the paranoia was because it was lethally contagious. The Jewish law even stated that lepers must repeatedly announce themselves by screaming out, "Unclean! Unclean!" while in public.[6] Stop and think for a moment about what a lifetime of publicly identifying oneself that way would do to a person.

The day you were diagnosed with leprosy was the last day you made contact with another human being. The only saving grace was that you wouldn't last in public for a lifetime. As soon as word got out, you'd be separated from your community and sent to live in a leper colony—a quarantined few acres reserved for the diseased to live and die with strangers with the same diagnosis.

To top it off, there was the spiritual component. Sadly, at this time in history, leprosy was believed to be evidence of God's judgment. The common belief was that every leper's skin was only the outward indication of their darkened soul. So a disease worn on the outside meant that onlookers would notice, and then they would judge: "This man committed some wrong so horrible that God inflicted permanent punishment on him." Now, this was, of course, a horribly abusive spiritual manipulation, but it was also quite common.

Lepers were banned from the temple as "unclean," meaning unfit for entry. That was a significant pronouncement because the temple represented two things in the first century—the presence of God and the epicenter of public society.

This was more than just a building for worship; it was rumored to be the actual house of God, meaning the place where his presence quite literally dwelt, the one and only place where God could be accessed. To be banned from the temple was to be told by (likely) the only spiritual authority you'll ever know, "Not you. This is not for you. You're too far gone—beyond redemption."

The temple was even more than a place of worship though; it was the marketplace of public society. Jerusalem's synagogue was like city hall with a chapel in it. It was the court, the grocery store, and the bank all in one. Functioning in society, regardless of views on divinity, required coming and going from the temple regularly. To be expelled meant not just spiritual banishment; it meant being permanently dispelled from civilization.

And that's exactly what happened. Lepers were cut off, left to suffer an incurable disease in a quarantined colony of the cursed. Sent away wondering what they had done to offend their Creator so deeply. The isolation was just as terminal as the swollen, wounded skin.

Think of everything behind the leper's statement to Jesus— "Lord, if you are willing, you can make me clean." That's temple language. "Make me clean" is Jewish religious language for the cleansing of sin. This is the request of a terminally ill man made to believe his offense toward God is the cause of his illness.

So Jesus reached down to this kneeling man and touched him. Before anything else, he touched him. I wonder when he had last been touched. I wonder what the throng following Jesus, their heads still spinning at his radical new teaching, thought when he reached out to touch a leper. I wonder if anyone tried to stop him. I wonder if anyone turned their face away in disgust. Jesus didn't. With compassion and dignity, Jesus looked into the knotted, warped skin that had once been pulled tight across this man's face.

Before Jesus "fixes" this man, he welcomes him. Gregory Boyle writes, "The principal cause of suffering for the leper is not an annoying, smelly, itchy skin disease but rather having to live outside the camp. So the call is to stand with them, so that the margins get erased and they are welcomed back inside."[7] And that's what Jesus did first—he erased the margins by welcoming this man before he qualified him by anyone else's standard.

Then he healed him, but you probably saw that part coming, and that's not really the best part anyway. The best part is the instruction after the healing:

> "Go, show yourself to the priest and offer the gift Moses commanded, as a testimony to them."
>
> *Matthew 8:4*

The gift Moses commanded? That's a gift of reinstatement into the temple. Jesus is saying, "Go back to your community. I haven't only healed you physically. I've made you clean. All the excuses people have used to cut you off, to draw a distance between you and them, every justification for isolation and division, that's all gone now. Go back home. Hug your family. Laugh with your friends. Know the joy of other people again, but be sure to follow the rules of the priests on reentry. Be sure they know you're back and there's nothing they can do to exclude you anymore. Be sure they know God isn't punishing you and never was. Be sure they know that God doesn't see 'clean' the way they see clean. Be sure there's no cheaper authority that will ever tear apart what I've put back together."

Jesus recovered the plot for the sexually shamed. Jesus recovered the plot for the diseased, judged, and outcast. Is anyone on the outside of his story? Who could possibly be lower than a prostitute and a leper?

Tax Collectors

The very bottom rung of the very lowest bar on the Hebrew moral scale belonged to tax collectors. By the time Jesus came around, Rome had essentially colonized Israel, and in Roman society, the elite class (roughly the top 2 percent) weren't taxed.[8] The remaining 98 percent were taxed heavily enough to ensure no one would be moving between peasant and elite status by their own merit. In the words of Cicero, "It is necessary that the distinctions of rank should be observed."[9]

The wealthy weren't taxed; they were the beneficiaries of taxes. But this was before W-2s and 1099 forms, and the wealthy weren't going door-to-door collecting taxes either. They hired that part out to the locals and sweetened the deal with a lavish, steady salary. Jews were hired by the Romans to collect Roman taxes from the conquered Jewish people. To be a tax collector was to trade teams, to move from being oppressed to doing the oppressing.

Tax collectors were people who weighed the pros and cons and chose personal wealth and comfort over loyalty and family. They had lived on the side of the victim, poked and prodded like animals, doing hard manual labor for minimum wage and then taxed on that income to such a high degree that they survived each month by the skin of their teeth.

All that changed the day you joined the enemy, which made you the wealthiest person in the village. Not only would you get a comfortable salary from the Roman elite, but Jewish tax collectors were famous for taking an extra cut for themselves on top of the exorbitant tax rate. No one received a written notice in the mail from the IRS. You just had to take the man's word for it. "If that's what I gotta pay, I guess that's what I gotta pay." Stealing was too easy for tax collectors. All they had to do was include the tip in the bill.

So if you're keeping score, 98 percent of the population is paid minimally for the hardest work and then taxed by a system carefully designed to keep the peasants poor and the elite rich. Then they are additionally taxed by their first cousin, who has joined the enemy and, as a result, is now the wealthiest guy in the village. That last part—that was the unforgivable sin.

You can hear the priest's voice bouncing off the echoing sanctuary walls: "Get out of this temple and never, ever set foot in here again!" Rejection is a gut punch under any circumstances, but this rebuke must've felt particularly sharp in a largely illiterate society some fifteen hundred years before the printing press. Under those conditions, the only way to hear the Word of God, to know the love and redemption of the Creator, was to hear it read by the priest in the temple. That voice of authority (God's authority!) is now saying, "No. Not you. This isn't for you. You're unforgivable."

■   ■   ■

One day, as Jesus walked along the shoreline, again a large crowd swarmed him. As he pushed through the crowd, he saw Levi sitting at the tax collector's booth, positioned just off the dock, to collect taxes on fish caught in waters that had been recently rebranded as "Roman-occupied." Several of Jesus' disciples were fishermen and probably knew Levi. They paid him on each day's haul. Jesus surprised everyone, maybe especially those closest disciples, when he stopped right in front of the tax booth, looked at Levi, and simply said, "Follow me."[10]

This was likely the first time Levi had been spoken to by a Jewish rabbi since his profession went public. He was stunned and flattered, but most of all, he was dignified to be seen for something more than the booth that wrapped itself around him like a giant name tag.

One thing led to another, and Jesus appeared at Levi's house for dinner. Levi invited all of his friends to meet this renegade rabbi who changed his life. His friends were all, of course, tax collectors. So Jesus sat on the front porch of the largest house in town, eating pita and baba ghanoush with the most hated people in all the surrounding villages. The priests got wind of the scene and rushed out to get a look for themselves. One of the priests tapped a couple disciples on the shoulder. "What's the deal with your rabbi? Why does he insist on breaking bread with tax collectors and sinners?"

When Jesus heard this, he said to them, "It is not the healthy who need a doctor, but the sick. I have not come to call the righteous, but sinners."[11]

Plenty has been written, and rightfully so, about Jesus' penchant for the poor, but what makes Jesus so different from many other revolutionaries is that he's equally merciful to the inner poverty of the uber-wealthy and highly accomplished. Beneath the comfortable home, high-class dinner parties, and peripheral access to the powerful Romans, there was a deep loneliness and inner poverty for the tax collector. Thomas Kelly refers to this as the tendered soul: "The hard-lined face of a money-bitten financier is as deeply touching to the *tendered* soul as are the burned-out eyes of miners' children, remote and unseen victims of his so-called success."[12]

Right into that emptiness, carefully disguised in prestige and success, Jesus spoke a better story. He spoke freedom to the captivity of trading everything for a position and reputation and still being eaten alive by emptiness and anxiety.

In the company of Jesus, the rich and poor are both welcome. Jesus' compassion reaches the obvious ills of the prostitute turning a trick and the ailing beggar, but it also reaches the hidden pain of inner emptiness within the outwardly successful. The compassion of Jesus knows no categories. He looks with affection on the oppressed and, potentially even more shockingly, on the incidental oppressor. Jesus recovered a plot so rich that it did more than dignify various people groups; it made them family again.

IMPRESSED BY THE UNIMPRESSIVE

Every account of Jesus' life is peppered with prostitutes, lepers, and tax collectors. Those most excluded by the unwritten rules of the day were most included in his inner circle. He shares meals with prostitutes publicly, lays his hands on the diseased skin of lepers, and even includes a rehabilitated tax collector among his twelve most trusted disciples. Jesus surrounded himself with all the wrong people.

It's like the societal lines that were so plain to everyone else were invisible to Jesus. He sought out the people most obviously injured by their society, the people who were told they weren't valuable, didn't matter, and were too far gone for redemption— the discarded ones. Repeatedly, he found ways to say to them, "You are my brothers and sisters." Brennan Manning writes, "One of the mysteries of the gospel tradition is this strange attraction of Jesus for the unattractive, this strange desire for the undesirable, this strange love for the unlovely."[13] Jesus surrounded himself with the leftovers and built a movement on the excluded.

Jesus showed up in a world with a carefully ordered social scale, a world where everyone else was content to play by the rules, and then flipped the whole thing on its head. He was confronting the whole system, calling into question the way value was given and taken in the first place.

The full implications of Jesus' life move all the way up to the possessors of power and position in his society—the priests. To associate with Jesus, to glimpse the rumored Messiah and question the leader of the greatest religious uprising in history, the elite Pharisee was forced to associate with the very people he disdained. The priest with a question for Jesus must squeeze between a couple of prostitutes in the mob surrounding him, rub shoulders with a throng of lepers as he moved toward the man at the center, and then finally take a seat on the ground next to the tax collector he had banished from his own temple pew.

Jesus was inviting those who were told they were nothing and those told they had made it, the possessors of shame and scandal and the possessors of image and prestige, to be seen for something other than their position. He was inviting them beyond the fragile castles they had built for themselves. Jesus approached each of these people in the presence of the Pharisees as a way of inviting prostitutes, lepers, tax collectors, *and Pharisees* into his family, calling them all brothers and sisters.

John Ortberg comments, "One of the most impressive aspects of Jesus is how he was impressed by unimpressive people."[14] The most striking part of this observation is that it is not based solely on Jesus' words. Jesus didn't only preach a new social order in sermons; he created it through his life. The corruption of the temple wasn't, first and foremost, protested by Jesus' lips; it was exposed by his life.

COMMUNITY

Zadie Smith's breakthrough novel *White Teeth* tells the story of Samad Iqbal, a middle-aged Indian man who works nights waiting tables at a curry house in London. He hates it.

I've had plenty of jobs in the restaurant industry. When I moved to New York at the age of twenty-two, I worked my days at a church in Midtown and my nights at a restaurant in the East Village. I got home four nights a week at 2:00 a.m., feet throbbing and back aching. It was hard work.

"And would you like garlic or plain naan with that?"

Samad didn't immigrate to London to ask that question. He didn't grow up dreaming of asking that question to table after table six nights a week. This is not who he dreamed of becoming, but here he is, tying on the apron again. He hates the perception that comes from that apron. It minimizes him in the eyes of others.

He works a job with constant human interaction, but these interactions never humanize him. They never dignify him. They peel away his dignity, making him a character necessary for someone else's meal. That's it. There's much more to him than just the guy refilling your water glass, but that's all people ever see.

In one memorable scene, he imagines waiting tables with a sign hanging around his neck that reads, "I am not a waiter. I have been a student, a scientist, a soldier, my wife is called Alsana, we live in East London but we would like to move north. I am a Muslim but Allah has forsaken me or I have forsaken Allah, I'm not sure. I have a friend—Archie—and others. I am forty-nine but women still turn in the street. Sometimes."[15]

The subtext of Samad's daydream is familiar to all of us: I want to be known.

What Samad is longing for in the form of a billboard necklace is the core longing for every human being—to be known completely and loved completely. He is neither. The apron he wears reduces him from a human being with a past and a story—with broken dreams, disappointments, passion, and hope—to a necessary background character in someone else's meal. He feels unseen, unknown, unloved. If only there was a way to introduce his whole self to the table before asking if they prefer still or sparkling water, then he could be known and maybe even loved. That's what his daydream is all about.

We are all most terrified of being fully known, and yet we all long to be seen for who we are (not for who we try to make ourselves) and be loved for that person. We all long to know others this way and love others this way too. Authentic community—the sort where performance and status aren't needed, the sort that lasts beyond its well-intentioned start but grows and blooms into a mature, sustained love for the other—we all want that. We all long for it. A community that cuts through status to true belonging: only there can we truly be known and truly be loved. Only there can we truly know and truly love.

We all have a longing for an authentic sense of community. We all want to be seen beyond our pretending. We all want to let our guard down and be accepted. And we all want this community to last, for it to be more than a flash in a pan or a euphoric phase. We all want family in the truest and best sense of the word.

No matter what you think of Jesus' claims of divinity, this part of his life is universally admired. Through the simple means of friendship, he reunited a fractured world. But the two-thousand-year gap between him and us might give us a wide enough buffer to admire this part of his life without being confronted by it.

Leprosy has been mostly eradicated, particularly in the Western world, and we've found much more systematized and accountable ways to collect taxes, so maybe some of the universal admiration comes from the safe distance that allows us the assumption that we are on Jesus' side, that we (the good guys, of course) would never subtly but effectively divide the world by a social and moral grid.

I don't have to look very far to see the consequences of Adam's first accusation. I just have to look up from my table when I'm out to dinner to notice that the front of the house staff (hostess and servers) are almost always people who look like me—white—and the back of house (cooks and dishwasher) are almost always people who don't look like me—people of color.

There are First and Third World countries around the globe, but in my city alone, I see waterfront high-rises, with more amenities than anyone could ever use, next door to government housing projects filled with first-generation immigrants eking out a living in a building that often smells of urine and tends to resemble a minimum security prison.

There are different languages spoken by different people groups all over the world, but there are many people speaking the same language, occupying the same few miles, who never consider one another as potential friends because the norms of their lives do not overlap.

The modern world, led by my generation, loves the idea of community, but are we willing to pay the cost of community? I know we celebrate the idea, but do we actually want to live in a diversity of relationships that discomfort, challenge, and stretch us?

The sociologist Robert Bellah seems to think it's just a celebration of ideas. He says we are misusing the term *community*. What most modern people mean by *community* is actually just "lifestyle enclaves."

> Though the term "community" is widely and loosely used by Americans, and often in connection with lifestyle, we would like to reserve it for a more specific meaning. Whereas a community attempts to be an inclusive whole . . . lifestyle is fundamentally segmented and celebrates the narcissism of similarities. For this reason, we speak not of lifestyle communities . . . but of lifestyle enclaves. Such lifestyles are segmental in two senses. They involve only a segment of each individual, for they concern only private life, especially leisure and consumption. And they are segmental socially in that they include only those with a common lifestyle . . . We might consider the lifestyle enclave an appropriate form of collective support in an otherwise radically individualizing society.[16]

Community is a word typically used to mean "people who match my habits of leisure and consumption—the people I've found who unwind like me and indulge like me." Community gets reduced to people who like the same bands I do, plan travel to the same places I do, and have the same opinion of who should win Best Picture this year at the Oscars. The robust, radical, familial ideal of community has in our time somehow become people who start their workday at the same local coffee roaster as I do and their weekend at the same microbrewery, people who wear the same brands I do, whose general lifestyle fits neatly and conveniently with mine. What we call "community" is usually just another grid to divide the world by a new set of criteria, and the modern criteria is painfully shallow—habits of leisure and consumption.

Dividing the world was intentional and came at a high cost. Slavery, racism, classism, sexism—all of these societal ills came when power was wielded by the insecure and fearful. Power is a dangerous thing if that power is not used in sacrificial love. The ripple effects of those divisions continue to plague our world in the forms of human trafficking, economic disparity, mass incarceration, workplace harassment, and the like. Maybe you and I didn't draw these lines, but we were born into a world where they were already drawn. We learned the lines without anyone explicitly teaching us. Jesus was born into a divided world that he personally didn't divide. He didn't help draw a single one of those lines, but he found a thousand ways to erase them.

Reuniting the world takes even more intention and probably a higher cost than dividing it. It's not enough to celebrate the "idea" of other people. We have to say yes to these other people on a personal, individual level. Right in the middle of the Sermon on the Mount, Jesus' most famous block of teaching, he says, "Be perfect, therefore, as your heavenly Father is perfect."[17] At first glance, the standard seems unreachable, but this verse can also be translated, "Be compassionate, therefore, just as your heavenly Father is compassionate." In fact, it seems that Luke, remembering the same teaching, translates it in a similar way: "Be merciful, just as your Father is merciful."[18]

The Quakers have a famous saying: "An enemy is one whose story we have not heard."[19] To follow Jesus is to be ever curious about the other. It is to cultivate the habit of learning the story of the other. This is often inconvenient, but compassion is rarely convenient or comfortable. What we call *comfort* keeps us playing within the lines that Jesus blurred.

To join Jesus' mission of compassion is to have a dinner table that breaks racial, economic, and social barriers. It is to have a circle of friends that provokes compelling questions from your colleagues. It is as simple as listening to the other and as profound as recreating the world in the image of the Creator. The apostle John wrote, "God is love,"[20] but the kind of love he named God is *agape*. God is family, so when we recreate that family on earth, we participate in God.

Unfortunately, the American church remains one of the most divided spheres in our society. This grieves the heart of God. One of the best memories I hold as a pastor came when Kirsten was pregnant with our first child. Jazmin invited us over for dinner. Jazmin is a single mother of four boys who lives in government subsidized housing. Her total household income is less than $10,000 a year (to support her family of five).

We pushed open her apartment door and were greeted by a choir of excited screams. "Surprise!"

Jazmin had planned a surprise baby shower for us. In that room were faces reflecting every shade. There were residents of luxury condos, trendy lofts, and housing projects. There were web developers, stockbrokers, artists, teachers, nurses, and the unemployed. Jazmin prepared a Puerto Rican feast like she would've done for a member of her own family, spending her limited income on the rest of us like it was never hers in the first place.

It was *agape*—a participation in the very person of God. And every time I slip those Jordan Brand socks on Hank's little feet—socks that aren't my taste but are precious because Jazmin picked them out—I think of that evening of *agape*. I got a glimpse at what a dinner party with Jesus must've felt like.

That's the formula: we join Jesus in erasing the lines that divide us in moments like that—as common as baby showers and as profound as re-creation.

Jesus spoke a better story into a world that had lost its way, to people who had managed to fracture society into plenty of tiny little pieces. Jesus still speaks to those of us who inherited a fractured world but struggle to leave it better than we found it, ironically blaming other people for the still-spreading cracks. Jesus reminds us who our neighbor is with the words on his lips, but that was only the beginning.

Much more profoundly, Jesus shows us who our neighbor is with the actions of his life. He didn't love the "idea" of other people; he actually loved the many individual people his life came into contact with. He didn't celebrate the sentiment of community. He created a family with prostitutes, lepers, tax collectors, and often confused but passionate disciples. He recovered the plot.

CHAPTER TEN

WORLD: A CURSE SOAKED INTO THE SOIL

"Cursed is the ground because of you . . .
for dust you are
*   and to dust you will return."*
Genesis 3:17, 19

Those two phrases bookend the consequences of sin. The infection is so personal. We express it in our unknown or unnamed emotions. We feel it in our most secret places—in our insecurity, competition, inadequacy, jealousy.

And yet the infection is equally universal. The consequences are in the ground we all walk on, the air we all breath, and, ultimately, in the end we all know is coming. We feel the consequences in disease, sickness, disability, and pain. The consequences of sin are universal, and death is the most obvious proof of that.

The point of this "cursed ground" is that suffering was not God's idea. Cancer, natural disasters, broken bones, and sinus infections—these and everything like them were not God's ideas. They are consequences, horrible consequences, that God is fighting against. This fight is so universal it's expressed in supernatural, miraculous power, but that fight is also so personal it involved God himself, feeling pain, sickness, grief, and suffering.

A FUNERAL PROCESSION

In his gospel, Luke writes, "Soon afterward, Jesus went to a town called Nain, and his disciples and a large crowd went along with him."[1] On his way through the city gates, Jesus had to stop and wait. There was a funeral procession. A couple of pallbearers covered in flowers inched out, followed by a priest in traditional vestments clutching a scroll with his head bowed. Then came the family. There weren't many of them, and they were all old. Last in line was a woman. She wasn't crying; she was wailing. She could hardly function. It was gut-wrenching to watch. She was followed only by a casket, carried on the shoulders of four pallbearers.

It was more of a small town than a big city, so it only took a bit of whispering to find out that the wailing woman was a widow with only one son. Her only son was in the casket. No one knew how he died. The family kept it quiet. All they knew was that it was a surprise to everyone.

Jesus couldn't take it anymore. He couldn't watch this. His heart broke with hers so completely that everything else faded to a blur and only she was in focus. "Don't cry," he blurted out.[2] Everything came back into focus, and he was in the center of it all. Profoundly moved by compassion, he had stopped the funeral procession of a complete stranger. There was no turning back now—he was right in the middle of it.

"Young man, I say to you, get up!"[3] A teenage boy sat upright in his casket. Terrified and delighted at the same time, three of the four pallbearers threw the casket off their shoulders, turning it over and spilling the boy into the dust. His mom hugged him, but it looked more like a mugging. She tackled him. She laughed hysterically. Pain in its rawest form had suddenly given way to joy in its rawest form. All eyes shifted over to Jesus.

Luke's gospel contains the only mention of the town of Nain anywhere in the Bible. We know very little of Jesus' ministry there. We know nothing about his success as a preacher in their temple or the possible presence of a church there in the years that followed his visit. The clearest manifestation of God's kingdom and character in Nain didn't end with an altar call or a Communion wafer or a book of daily readings to discuss with a few close friends. When God showed up in Nain, it looked like a teenage boy sitting up in his casket. It looked like healing for a family that most likely had long ago given up on healing and was grieving the cursed ground they were stuck on. It looked like healing for a family that wasn't asking for it, and as far as we can tell wasn't looking for it. It looked like indescribable joy for a mother who gave no indication she had any hope left or believed healing was possible, that she, or anyone else in Nain, for that matter, even knew who Jesus was.

A question I often ask myself as a pastor is, *If our church shut its doors tomorrow, if all of our activity ceased, would Brooklyn even notice? Would the city be different at all if this church weren't in it?* The reason I think this is a question worth asking is that if you ask it of any village Jesus ever set foot in, the answer would be, "Yes, a lot of people would notice because a lot of people would be a whole lot worse off."

From what I can tell, the main difference between Jesus and the modern church is the effect each has on the larger community—particularly the community that doesn't participate in the rituals of gathered worship, those potentially open to the church's help but uninterested in the church's teaching.

We don't know what the citizens of Nain thought of what Jesus had to say. All we know for sure is that everyone was

glad he came. Everyone—the priest at the head of the proces-
sional, the self-absorbed businessman annoyed at the length of
time the town gate was clogged up, the pallbearer angry and
confused about what had happened to his friend, the mother
weeping hysterically, and the teenage boy who suddenly had
days ahead of him again. Jesus was a welcomed addition for
everyone because he had come to repair a broken creation, and
that affects everyone.

When Jesus showed up in a new city, it was good news
for everybody—those in the temple every day and those who
weren't interested in setting foot in that building. Jesus was a
welcomed intrusion for those who believed and those who never
would, for those hanging on his every word and those who stood
at the fringe, wondering what the commotion was all about and
who walked away annoyed the second they heard the word *God*.

LUNCH FOR FIVE THOUSAND

There's one miracle, only one, that's recorded by all four gospels.[4] At the end of a couple of days of teaching and listening and
helping the many people who followed him around like sheep
follow a shepherd, Jesus knew they must be hungry. Actually,
his disciples brought that fact up to him, probably because *they*
were hungry. I would've been too.

Jesus had them scavenge through the crowd in search of food.
Philip found a kid who had a stash of five stale rolls and a couple
of cans of tuna. "Great. This'll work." Jesus had them sit in
groups to make the food distribution orderly and efficient, like
a big wedding with only one buffet table. He prayed and gave
thanks to *Abba* for the food they were all about to eat.

While he was praying, the disciples didn't bow their heads.
They were sneaking glances at each other. *Has the heat gotten
to him? There's not enough for everyone to have a nibble. How's*

he planning on making this work? No one spoke up, but their bewildered looks said it all.

These were fair questions to ask. During the seating arrangements, the disciples had tallied five thousand men, meaning five thousand households. There were stadiums that didn't have the seating capacity for this crowd, and this guy was holding one brown bag lunch.

Jesus handed out the food so fast they didn't know who had what; he sent each of the twelve disciples to different groups. Everyone ate until they couldn't stomach another bite. People were so bloated they lay down, totally horizontal, on the grass. Not sure when the next time they'd come across such a promising lunch, Jesus sent the same disciples back through the crowd to collect leftovers—twelve basketfuls. That seemingly insignificant detail is actually the clue that grounds this miraculous story in the context of the larger plot. Jesus is feeding the hungry, but the twelve basketfuls reveal the larger story the feast points to.

IS THAT IT?

Many of the people I talk to about God were handed a version of the gospel story that ends with God saving a few souls, getting as many of us off this sinking ship as he can before this thing goes down. This version has a kernel of truth in it that some grasp on to for dear life. But then, maybe a couple months, maybe a couple years, maybe a couple decades in, they ask, "Is that it? Is that really the grand plan of God? Is that really what this whole world, this whole life, comes down to?"

No, that's not it. Or perhaps I should say, that is a tiny minimization of what "it" is. The world is definitely broken, but Jesus isn't trying to whisk away enough souls to populate a far-off utopia called heaven; he's trying to bring heaven to earth.

The healings of Jesus tell us that. They tell us there's more than just a solution to all your problems that will kick in when you die.

Before the ground was cursed, the Creator spoke purpose over creation:

> "Be fruitful and increase in number; fill the earth and sub-
> due it. Rule over the fish in the sea and the birds in the sky
> and over every living creature that moves on the ground."
>
> *Genesis 1:28*

People, made in the image of God, were given authority over creation, to "rule" over it with wisdom and generosity.

Sin was the mismanagement of a God-given position of authority. Then Jesus showed up healing—ruling creation with the wisdom and generosity intended at the beginning, exemplifying the life you and I were always meant to know.

Jesus healed the sick, exemplifying authority over physical disease and disability.[5]

Jesus calmed the storm, exemplifying authority over nature.[6]

Jesus raised Lazarus, exemplifying authority over death.[7]

Jesus wasn't healing for the sake of spectacle. He wasn't doing a few magic tricks to increase the attendance on his preaching tour. He wasn't working miracles to prove he was worth believing. He was undoing the curse that had soaked all the way into the soil. He was reversing the effects of sin.

Jesus broke bread for five thousand people, but that wasn't to show off how effortless catering is for God. That act was a promise to restore everything that was lost.

Twelve disciples waited tables. Twelve baskets of leftovers were collected. Twelve tribes made up the nation of Israel, God's covenant people.

The symbolism is obvious. "There's more than enough for everyone." That's what Jesus is saying through this miracle.

On an ordinary day in Israel, Jesus used the giving of food to redeem what was lost on an ordinary day in Eden through the taking of food.

John, one of the men collecting leftovers that day, remembered the rumors that swept through the crowd:

"Surely this is the Prophet who is to come into the world."

John 6:14

In other words, "Surely this is how it was always supposed to be. Surely this is the plot our lives were meant to be lived within all along. Surely this man is recovering all that was lost." And he was. And he is.

CHAPTER ELEVEN

RECOVERING THE PLOT

The English novelist E. M. Forster draws a distinction between a story and a plot with the single word *because*. A story is merely events arranged chronologically—"the king died and then the queen died." A plot occurs when the focus zeroes in on the causality, the *because*, of those events—"the king died, and then the queen died of grief."[1]

The question Jesus' life leaves us with is this: Is it merely a story, or is it a plot? Is his life only a series of events, or is it something more coherent, the first and greatest *because*?

To answer this question, we are forced to engage a similar, but much more personal question: Is my life merely a story, or is it a plot? Am I the sum total of chronological events, or is there a coherent plot?

Frederick Buechner opens his final of three memoirs juggling that very question and drawing this conclusion: "I can say only that to me life in general, including my life in particular, *feels* like a plot, and I find that a source both of strength and of fascination."[2] I would add to his words that the life of Jesus is the only *because* I've found to be big enough, real enough, and true enough to make sense of the story I find myself living—to turn my story into a plot.

GOOD NEWS

Jesus called his own life and message "good news."[3] Why? Because the God whom Jesus revealed is big enough to paint the stars across the sky with a single word from his lips and personal enough for an unhurried conversation with a single individual. The incomprehensible Maker of the cosmos is also gentle, loving, and personal. He is powerful enough to calm the storm and personal enough to patiently, presently listen with compassion in his eyes to the insecurities and fears of a single individual. He is powerful enough to heal the sick and personal enough to weep alongside the grieving. He is powerful enough to feed the nations and personal enough to pass the rolls across the common table.

His redemption is too big for human power alone and so personal that it includes every last one of us—the legalistic priest in formal robes and the leper who is refused entry; the lost son at rock bottom and the outwardly successful, inwardly empty older brother; the weeping mother at the grave and the teenage boy carrying lunch to his summer job. Jesus' message is good news because it's the only plot big enough for the complexity of the world and personal enough for me and you to catch and join.

In an "eye for an eye" society built on fairness and rights, Jesus forgave when he was wronged without demanding a return. That's good news for every offender. He set people free from owing any debt.

At a time in history when ailments were thought of as curses from God, signs of condemnation, Jesus healed the sick, gave sight to the blind, cleansed the skin of those with leprosy, and made the paralyzed to stand. That's good news for the excluded. He restored people to the community they were created to enjoy.

In a society heavily based on class and power, Jesus dignified the outcast, the overlooked, the condemned, and the forgotten by treating them as equal—better than equal—as honored. That's good news for the marginalized. To those worthless in this world, he gives divine worth.

His teaching wasn't eloquent or well-rehearsed. It was something better. It was true. That's good news for those reaching for control through perfection. The life that humanity lost through control is restored through surrender.

Jesus loves relentlessly. His love can't be broken. He was ignored, opposed, cursed, even betrayed. None of it changed his fixed gaze of love. That's good news for everybody, every last one of us. Jesus, by love, restores the trust humanity lost in the Creator of this story gone mad.

The Bible isn't the only story. There are plenty of other stories painting different portraits of an all-powerful Designer with exclusive truth claims. The myriad of available religious, mystical, and philosophical stories makes this absolutely clear: An all-powerful Creator is not necessarily "good news." It all depends on what the Creator does with all that power.

The life of Jesus claims that the all-powerful God of the universe is loving, kind, and merciful. He is for you, not against you. In Jesus, God undressed himself of every speck of divinity that might separate you from him. He came down to our level. He lived among us. Faced what we face. Was tempted as we are. Took on pain as we must. He humbled himself, weakened himself, emptied himself—all for the sake of one loving pursuit: a restored relationship with you.[4]

Richard Foster writes, "Humility means to live as close to the truth as possible: the truth about ourselves, the truth about others, the truth about the world in which we live . . . Humility is, in fact, filled with power to bring forth life. The word itself comes from the Latin *humus*, which means fertile ground."[5]

Jesus showed us a new way to live. Actually, he reminded us of the life we were always meant to live but had lost somewhere along the way. That's why, as much as you cringe at the way Jesus is portrayed in mass media—as detestable as it may be to think about some of his most outspoken representatives, and as muddled as his reputation may be because of your personal and painful past experience—when you take a hard, honest look at the life of Jesus of Nazareth, something comes alive in you, some sort of longing, some sort of homesickness. His life awakens you; it pulls at you. And that's only because he's living the truth—the truth about God, about the self, about other people, and about the world.

Here is the life of Jesus: the director inserted himself into the story, and he has recovered the plot.

CHAPTER TWELVE

A WAY TO DIE

Read the biography of any famous person, and the author will always focus on that person's life. There will be chapter after chapter after chapter on their childhood, the circumstances of their development, and the major accomplishments of their life. Then the whole thing wraps up with a little sliver on their death and a line or two about legacy. As John Ortberg writes, "If you read the biography of any famous person, even if their death was a prominent story (for example, Abraham Lincoln, Mahatma Gandhi, Martin Luther King Jr.), it will be only a tiny part of that biography."[1]

While training for the one and only marathon I've ever run, I distracted myself from counting miles by listening to the audiobook of Martin Luther King Jr.'s autobiography.[2] It was insightful, rich, inspiring, and full of anecdotes about King's life I'd never heard. It was the best kind of "long read." I was lost in it.

Then it ended as startlingly as a dark indie film. You're completely lost in the story, unsure of where it's going but unable to look away, and then the credits just roll. That's it? I knew the end of Dr. King's story. He was famously and tragically assassinated by James Earl Ray in Memphis on April 4, 1968. His life was cut tragically short, and his death still echoes through history. But those who have devoted decades to studying and understanding him do not attribute great meaning to his death. His life is wrung out in thousands of words on thousands of pages, but his death is briefly summarized as a tragic interruption to an otherwise brilliant story.

All four reputable biographies of Jesus' life work the opposite way. His death takes up a disproportionate amount of real estate—roughly one-third of each gospel. There's very little on his childhood and next to nothing on the circumstances of his development. The accounts can't seem to agree on the key moments to highlight from his life, as each one is made up of a different list of his miracles and teachings. But all four accounts slow way down in Jesus' final week. They all fall into perfect harmony with one another, suddenly documenting each precise detail when they had been a sweeping survey up to that point. Every one of Jesus' biographers seemed to recognize that something significant was happening in his death.

Jesus didn't come only to show us how to live. If all that had gone wrong was that we had lost our way, God could've just sent a map. If the world was broken and in need of fixing, why didn't God just send down an instruction manual? What sort of circumstances could be so dire as to require God to enter the story and die?

God came as a human being because we didn't just need missing information; we had a debt to pay. The choice to put the self at the center is a transaction in hope. To place the self at the center, to sit down on the throne of your own life, is creation saying to Creator, "Thanks for the boost. I'll take it from here."

I'll find my own fulfillment.

I'll construct my own identity.

I'll write a story big enough to satisfy my own soul.

That choice ripped a separation between creation and Creator. God is the author of life, the inventor of existence. God, in his very nature, is life. Any attempt at life without God is, by its very nature, death. Life on my terms results in death. There is no possible reordering of these terms that results in full, lasting life. The breach between Creator and creation cannot be closed by creation, but only by the Creator.

So how do we close a gap opened up through putting the self at the center—the definitive act of selfishness? It takes the definitive act of selflessness—laying down the perfect life. We needed more than an instruction manual, so God came as a person. But why, then, did God need to live thirty-three years before death, if death was really the big moment, the big payoff, anyway? Because life had to be lived according to design, without sin. The plot had to be recovered by truly living, by going through the ordinary days of ordinary life in this very flawed world, but doing it all in such a way that God maintained his place at the center.

For every day of Jesus' life, God was his protector, provider, and the recipient of his exaltation. Another way of saying this is that Jesus lived without sin—and remember, I don't primarily mean Jesus never told a lie, watched pornography in middle school, and got blackout drunk on prom night (Jesus didn't do any of those things, but sin isn't exclusively about morality). I also don't mean that Jesus avoided ever choosing, even for a second, the self for the center (though, again, he did avoid ever doing that, but to focus on what Jesus didn't do is to miss the point entirely).

Jesus lived without sin, and that means that every moment of every day he chose God as the center of his life. Instead of the charade of trying to insulate himself with enough comfort and security that he could feel free, he lived freely by accepting God as his protector. Instead of the futility of human attempts at control, he chose God as his provider. Instead of the exhaustion of making a name for himself, he took the name God gave him and pointed at the giver of names.

Jesus lived. He really lived. He lived like we were always meant to live. He lived full and abundant and whole. And he did it all so he could die, really die, die the death we were always meant to die, die completely and fully and finally.

Jesus lived without sin, and that meant he had no abrupt ending coming his way. There was no inevitable death awaiting Jesus. We go kicking and screaming to our death, fighting against that dimming light until our final breath, but Jesus' death was nothing like that. He had to lay his life down, choosing death voluntarily. There was no fighting. There was no dimming light. Death had no hold on him. He chose to die.

That's what it took to pay the debt. It took a supernatural life in a natural world, choosing to die willingly in place of a bunch of souls that had chosen death before realizing the magnitude of the choice. When Jesus chose death, he was choosing life for you and me.

Henri Nouwen said it well: "Yes, there is such a thing as a good death. We ourselves are responsible for the way we die. We have to choose between clinging to life in such a way that death becomes nothing but a failure, or letting go of life in freedom so that we can be given to others as a source of hope."[3]

Jesus did not fight the dying light. He was living in only light and chose to dive headfirst into darkness. Why did he do it? He let go of his free life so we could hope again. He was opening up the possibility for us to reverse the exchange, to return our hope to God, to accept his offer to pay the debt we couldn't pay. He took on death so you and I wouldn't have to.

THE GIFT OF PASSIVITY

When we remember Jesus, we typically think of his birth, life, and death as one sweeping divine act. We rarely distinguish between the life of God and the death of God, imagining the whole thing as one neatly packaged divine gift. In fact, Jesus gave us two great gifts—his life and his death. In the words of

Ronald Rolheiser, "Jesus gave his life for us in one way, through his activity; he gave his death for us in another way, through his passivity, his passion."[4]

Typically, when people speak of the "passion of Jesus Christ," they are intending to make much of the brutal suffering. They're making a summary reference to whips that bring one to the brink of death but stop just short, forcing breath to keep flowing through a body that can no longer be called human. They're speaking of ruthless soldiers making evening plans while forcing thick iron nails through the wrists and feet of an innocent man. They're speaking of a spear just under the rib cage when the dying is dragging on so long that boredom is setting in. Make no mistake, Jesus' death was brutal, but the brutality of the way he died was not his passion; the passion of Jesus Christ was his free choice to die.

Rolheiser explains: "The English word *passion* takes its root in the Latin *passio*, meaning 'passivity,' and that is its primary connotation here: what the passion narratives describe for us is Jesus' passivity. He gives his death to us through his passivity, just as he had previously given his life to us through his activity."[5]

For thirty-three years, Jesus gave us his activity, his life. He was always active, always doing—teaching, healing, advocating, feeding, freeing, including, comforting, noticing, inviting, hoping, instructing, loving.

His final twenty-four hours represented a distinct shift, obvious to every close observer. Beginning with his arrest in Gethsemane, Jesus gave us his passivity, his death. Every gospel author's description of Jesus takes an obvious grammatical turn at that point—all the verbs become passive. He is led away. He is questioned. He is tortured. He is whipped. He is mocked. He is provided help in carrying his cross. He is nailed to it.

He is no longer doing; he is allowing to be done. He is no longer acting; he is being acted upon.

When people question God, it's always related to his activity.

What was God doing when that happened to me? Where was God when I really needed help? How could a loving God willingly allow this in my life [or her life or his life or our lives]? Why did God act in this way? Why didn't God act in this way?

As people who often demand more action, more doing from God, this simple fact is worth consideration: The greatest gift God ever gave us was his passivity, not his activity; his restraint, not his action. It was his willingness to be acted on without intervention. It was his chosen powerlessness, not his power. It was not his doing, but his allowing. It is the passivity of God that is most revealing of his character. In Jesus' passion, he gave us a gift we could not receive by his action.

Mark's account includes the reaction of the centurion, the Roman army commander who oversaw the execution. When the last breath left Jesus' body, when the gift of love was completely given through divine restraint, the centurion said aloud, "Surely this man was the Son of God!"[6]

This Jewish rabbi had walked all over the Roman Empire for three years, healing the sick, causing the paralyzed to stand, giving sight to the blind, straightening the backs of the disfigured, cleansing the skin of lepers, restoring the minds of the insane, and even raising the dead, but none of that looked like God to those in power. Somehow what they had missed in his power they saw in his restraint. The centurion recognized the divine bloodline in Jesus by his weakness, not his strength; his surrender, not his victory; his death, not his life; his love, not his power. There was something otherworldly, something wondrous, about the way he willingly gave up his life.

Jesus' most powerful healing came by dying. Pete Greig writes, "When Jesus cried out from the cross, 'It is finished,' he was declaring the death of death, the cure for suffering, the remission of sin. In that single moment, we were found . . . We were saved by the sacrifice of another."[7]

PITCH-BLACK

Scripture says that when Jesus was breathing his final breaths, in the middle of the day in the sun-scorched Middle East, the world got dark:

> From noon until three in the afternoon darkness came over all the land.
>
> *Matthew 27:45*

Don't you see it? The darkness isn't recurring anymore. The day God died, life no longer seemed wedged between light and dark—unfathomable potential and recurring darkness.

On that Friday afternoon, darkness was not a force nagging every human life, following us around like a looming cloud we couldn't quite outrun. On that day, darkness became a blanket. There were no pinpricks of light, no cracks in the door, no blades of light cutting through the room for the dust to dance in. Nothing. Pitch-black.

For about seventy-two hours, it seemed the darkness had won. But it was a short-lived victory.

CHAPTER THIRTEEN

A WAY TO LIVE AGAIN

A Sunday morning in Jerusalem—an otherwise ordinary morning. Peasants crowded the major intersections near the central marketplace, some arriving while it was still dark. A prime position was key for getting picked up as a day laborer, and fifteen hours under the melting sun among the livestock of a complete stranger—that's another day of survival.

The minutes tick by slowly now for the Roman soldiers patrolling the streets. They always do just before a shift change. The rising light is hitting the sundial, and you just can't keep yourself from peeking at the shadow, constantly waiting for it to arrive at just the right angle. The daydreams of revelry and rest, now so close, always seem to slow the turning of time.

The Jewish priests are up early and light on their feet. They've got their temple back. It wasn't easy, and it wasn't particularly popular—at first. But they eventually won over the crowds. Hurling accusations, bending the revered scrolls, and spreading propaganda are all made a bit easier when you're the only educated ones among a mostly illiterate society. Complete control of the narrative made turning it against the wayward, gluttonous, indulgent rabbi too easy.

You know the next part. The tomb was empty. An event on an otherwise ordinary morning in a Roman-occupied Jewish city in the first century caused everyone to stop and wonder—the peasants awaiting a job and the landowners picking through the candidates, the Roman soldiers standing intimidatingly on every street corner and the Jewish priests carefully adorning themselves in robes and tassels, the disciples hiding in the upper room, and Pontius Pilate peeling himself out of bed—every last one of them, and everyone everywhere who would come after them, was suddenly interrupted in a way that left them speechless for a moment.

JESUS' MOST OFFENSIVE ACT

We could live with the resurrection as an exaggerated story intended to instill virtue in its hearers. If Jesus' resurrection was a metaphor, that makes him a likable revolutionary. It means we can learn from him; we can take from his life what might be helpful for ours. We can pick him over like any other historical figure, admiring him for his extraordinary character, memorializing the ways he was misunderstood in his time but now, in our more sophisticated, broadly progressive culture and with the benefit of hindsight, we can understand him properly, accurately gaining insight from him—a wise sage from another time offering us advice from a rocking chair but not understanding our iPhones, pace of life, or money made of pixels.

If the resurrection of Jesus was a metaphor, he was a prophet misunderstood in his time—Kurt Cobain with a more profound message. We can remember him for what he could've been, should've been, if he had been allowed to live a full life. We can take solace in the metaphorical resurrection, meaning his teachings never died and his spirit lived on in his few followers.

If the resurrection was a metaphor, Jesus was a teacher with depth and eloquence far too great for the ears of the common peasants he taught. He had a message to be pondered by the greats, and it was wasted on the uneducated, illiterate simpletons that surrounded him. He's Will Hunting with no Robin Williams to get him out of South Boston, so he did the best he could with the Affleck brothers.

A resurrection metaphor makes Jesus a philosopher on par with the likes of Socrates, Plato, Kant, and Kierkegaard. He's pulled something so profound from a left-brained mind, the right brains will teach it in classrooms for centuries to come.

A resurrection metaphor makes Jesus a social justice symbol. Actually, it makes him *the* social justice symbol. His life is the one that became the model for Gandhi, Nelson Mandela, and Martin Luther King Jr. to follow. His "resurrection" is the spirit of peaceful protest that has cut a better way through some of the harshest periods of oppression in history. His life is truly a light. His life has been a light in some of the darkest nights of world history—Indian poverty, South African apartheid, American slavery.

A resurrection metaphor is a way of saying that Jesus' virtue lives on, even now, in those he continues to influence, and that makes Jesus a great man. Maybe it even makes him the greatest man. A great man about whom we have much to admire. A great man we should always remember and never forget. A man so great he was even able to die an unjust death with grace and dignity. This is not an offensive figure, not one about whom people hold polarizing opinions, not one who divides people as "sheep and goats."[1]

Read back through the description above. Who finds there a man they disagree with or oppose? We would universally admire the Jesus of metaphorical resurrection. We'd make his life into books that fly off the shelves and movies with Sigur Rós soundtracks that build tears behind every set of eyes.

Even those who claim to believe in the resurrection intellectually probably don't in practice. Very few of us live in light of an actual resurrection. The theologian William Willimon puts it quite honestly:

I don't need a resurrected Jesus. Come to think of it, I'm not sure I *want* a resurrected Jesus . . . I have the illusion that I'm in control, that I am making a so significant contribution to help Jesus that I may be eternal on my own. No, I don't need a bodily resurrected Jesus. In fact, if I ever got one, my life would only become much more difficult.[2]

Here's what he's getting at. If Jesus showed us a new way to live and a better way to die, we are left to pick over his life like a swarm of vultures, gnawing at his bones for something of him we can add to ourselves. A Jesus of life and death is a fantastic addition. To this Jesus, we come with our already full lives, having already decided who we will be, where we will go, what we dream of, and what is needed to accomplish those dreams. We add this Jesus like milk in a cup of coffee—just a splash; there's not much room left, but I'd love to get that nice caramel color.

But an actual resurrection? That requires an empty cup, contents poured out until it's bare ceramic, so it can be filled to overflowing with living water.

You see, the resurrection is actually Jesus' most offensive act.

A bodily resurrection means Jesus isn't a likable revolutionary. He can't be. Kurt Cobain, Will Hunting, Gandhi, Mandela, MLK—none of those men walked out of their graves.

An actual resurrected Jesus does not make him a great man. It makes him Lord. It means he flooded the recurring darkness with constant light—overcame systemic evil, swallowed up personal failure, and defeated death. The parts of life so painful that the best we can do is "change the subject"—he cut a way through. If Jesus really rose, we fall on our knees in worship or stand up in offense because it means he is either Lord or thinks he is (and that's dangerous). If Jesus really rose, he is more than a great man—much more. He is Lord and God. That's what led the apostle Paul to claim that everything hangs on the resurrection.

> If Christ has not been raised, our preaching is useless and
> so is your faith.
>
> *1 Corinthians 15:14*

The novelist and screenwriter John Irving repeated the
sentiment: "Anyone can be sentimental about the Nativity; any
fool can feel like a Christian at Christmas. But Easter is the
main event; if you don't believe in the resurrection, you're not
a believer."[3]

BREATHING LIFE BACK INTO THE CAST

The life of Jesus was about recovering the plot of the story;
the resurrection of Jesus was about breathing life back into
the cast. When the tomb turned up empty and Jesus started
showing up, startling his disillusioned followers hiding out from
the authorities, he was giving them something entirely new,
releasing something into the world, setting it free to spread and
grow. Hope—that's what the resurrection and the fifty days of
appearances that followed it were all about. *Hope.*

Don't misunderstand me. I'm not talking about some fairy-
tale kind of hope. The very worst explanations of the resurrection, the ones that make you want to throw this book against
the wall and take a shower just to wash off whatever you picked
up from reading this far, sound like a fairy-tale ending: "Jesus'
resurrection means you get to start tucking your shirt in, get
the Lego man haircut, spend many hours of your precious life
in painfully boring church services, and then, when that abrupt
ending finally comes for you, you get whisked off to a better
world with Saint Peter and the gang." Relax. That's not what
I'm talking about.

Fairy-tale endings cheapen this life. Fairy-tale endings
aren't enough for disappointment, confusion, grief, unmet

expectations, unrequited longing, anger, poverty, suffering, and loss—the real substance of life, the stuff that puts us on our backs. Fairy-tale endings do nothing for that other than remind us we've got an express ticket already punched. They cheapen the complexity of this life.

Jesus' resurrection released hope, not to cheapen life in this world, but to dignify it. To believe in the resurrection is to place the full weight of my hope in the "story of Jesus." It is to acknowledge that at the center of the harsh reality of life, there is a supernatural gap that cannot be closed by my natural means.

A dignifying sort of hope sounds something like this: The universe we inhabit is the very good creation of a very good God who is deeply grieved by the darkness that haunts the lives of his children. This God is so relentless in unwavering hope and pursuing love that he stopped at nothing to heal and redeem us. He promises justice in place of every societal failure, and justice for every last victim. He promises forgiveness to cover over every personal failure, and freedom from the guilt and shame it drags behind. He promises that life, not death, will have the final word because death has once and for all been defeated.

A dignifying sort of hope is not a fairy-tale utopia you get swept off to when you're done grinding it out in the world you helped mess up. It means heaven is coming to earth. It means Jesus really was the last Adam, that just as the first Adam gave birth to death, Jesus gave birth to life. Hope means to begin living, even now, in that better story of Jesus, so that our very lives become a participation in the redemption of the world.

To borrow an idea from Philip Yancey, when it comes right down to it, there are really just two ways to look at human history.[4] We can focus on the brokenness. We can see the dysfunction of violence, oppression, war, abuse, and death. In that world, resurrection is nothing more than a moment of exception, when God stunningly contradicted every other pattern.

But there's a second way called hope. Hope means resurrection is a new starting point. It is the supreme picture of how God interacts with humanity, whom he loves. Hope makes resurrection the ultimate reality, and everything else is just the exception.

Hope that lives in you and me and anyone else who chooses it—that's what was released early one Sunday morning when the tomb was found empty. Jesus didn't walk out of his grave to cheapen this life with a first-class ticket to another world. He did it to dignify this life by bringing heaven to earth and to dignify you by giving you, right now in the midst of the mess, a unique, tailor-made, participatory role in that redemption.

Jesus doesn't have a monopoly on metanarrative. There are plenty of other origin stories that claim to explain this life and fill it with meaning. The compelling thing about Jesus is that his story starts with love, ends with love, and brings redemption through love. He offers us a story big enough to explain the complex mess we call the world, and powerful enough to redeem every square inch through love—the sort of love that never gives up, the sort of love that swallows up fear, the sort of love that heals, however quickly or slowly, the sort of love that outlasts the sting of pain.

When Andrew landed that role and started off on tour in the company of those who'd "made it" on the uber-exclusive Broadway stage, he thought he'd finally arrived at the chapter in his story that would feel like enough. It didn't. Only the story of Jesus supplies meaning enough to satisfy the eternity in the human soul. What he was in search of on stage after stage was hidden in plain sight all along.

When Cara had run the cycle of weekend escapes, casual sex, and heavy shame enough times to honestly confess, "I'm finding life in Brooklyn hugely unsatisfying," she was greeted by the love of Jesus. His love doesn't pretend. It doesn't go back and edit our stories so that the most painful moments never happened. It repurposes the moments we'd like to edit into the moments we treasure most because they are the ones overflowing with grace.

When Phil was trying to breathe through a panic attack because he thought he was leaving a job but it turned out he was shedding himself of a part of his identity he didn't know how to live without, he was gently invited to find a truer identity, given him first—one he didn't earn, would never find on a résumé, and could never lose.

When Jesus carried his own cross on his back, he was carrying more than a cross; he was carrying all of creation. He was carrying my story and yours. He was carrying the consequences of every human wrong and the weight of all the world's suffering.

Only Jesus offers a picture of love that is stronger than death. That's why an agonizing, public execution isn't a barbaric, outdated, grotesque religious idea; it's a stunning picture of love. And the claim of the resurrection is this: there is a kind of love that outlives death.

Jesus recovered the plot, and there's no other plot like it.

But for many, that's still not enough.

It's not enough because we aren't just confronting the cosmic problems of a world gone mad. That's certainly part of it, but that's not all of it.

It's much, much more personal than that.

Part 3

THE STORY OF
OUR TWIN

CHAPTER FOURTEEN

DIDYMUS

Maybe Jesus' followers wanted him to be divine so badly, wanted to believe anything but the truth with such rigor, that they ran with the most far-fetched, supernatural explanation of a very natural event.

The body's gone. That's historical fact.

The body's gone because it came back to life? . . . That's one theory.

Plenty of people have offered plenty of other theories, but they basically all boil down to some sort of grave robbing or Roman soldier conspiracy theory. I don't mean conspiracy theory in the "we never landed on the moon" or "Beyoncé and Jay-Z really control everything through the Illuminati" sense. I mean conspiracy theory in the "there has to be a practical explanation for what seems like a supernatural event" sense.

So maybe we look back on Jesus' followers with psychological pity. They wanted to believe the "Jesus rose" theory so badly that at the slightest inkling of evidence that could maybe, if they stretched it as far as it would go in just the right direction, confirm their belief, they just couldn't help themselves.

That would make a lot of sense, except that wasn't how Jesus' followers responded to his missing body. The first people to arrive at the empty tomb on that resurrection morning were much more realists than they were gullible fanatics.

Mary Magdalene was the first to arrive at the tomb. The Saturday prior was the Jewish Sabbath, so she was forced to wait twenty-four long hours to honor the loss of her rabbi, according to custom. The Jewish people had a much more elaborate grieving process than modern Westerners. They clothed themselves in garments of sackcloth and sprinkled ashes on their foreheads and put anointing spices on the body of the deceased.

"For dust you are, and to dust you will return."[1] *Our rabbi has returned to the dust*, Mary Magdalene thought. *It's time to mourn completely, feel the loss and disappointment all the way through, so eventually we can lift up our heads and keep moving.* Honoring the Sabbath, the highest of Jewish traditions, she hadn't dared do the "work" of grieving on Saturday—clothing the tomb with the scent of anointing oil and spices, adorning it with flowers. Even a revolutionary, irreverent rabbi like Jesus wouldn't have wanted that.

While the rest of Jerusalem slept, she was lying awake in an upper room the rest of them had all been content to hide out in, but not her. She was stir-crazy. So the second the first ember of burning light appeared over the horizon, she was walking the dusty road back up the familiar hill she had watched Jesus walk, carrying his own cross, seventy-two hours ago. That walk must've made the nightmare she had already relived in her thoughts a hundred times feel that much more real, that much more final. "He really is gone. It really is over. The brakes have squealed to a full stop on all of our dreaming. I guess this is what moving on feels like."

She noticed the stone rolled away from a distance. What were her first thoughts? *Oh no, those terrible soldiers are making a mockery of him again! Maybe they're forcing another crown of thorns on his deceased skull! They wouldn't make a dead body into a toy, would they? They would. Maybe they're knocking him around, telling him to prophesy again. Or maybe they're trying to profit. They auctioned off his cloak to the highest bidder within thirty seconds of his last breath. Would they really remove the loincloths from his waist and do the same? They would. They're ruthless.*

She hurried her pace while her mind ran faster.

She got there, and he was gone. Here are the first recorded words from her mouth:

> "They have taken the Lord out of the tomb, and we don't know where they have put him!"
>
> *John 20:2*

She raced back to the secret, second-floor hideaway and said this to Peter. He was the first of the twelve to wake up that morning.

"They have taken the Lord out of the tomb, and we don't know where they have put him!" These are not the words of a gullible fanatic; they're the words of a realist. She's not imagining fantastic scenarios; she's imagining very realistic, very logical ones. On resurrection morning, Mary Magdalene was not living in a fantasy world. She had two feet firmly planted on earthly soil, living in the story of this world—where death is abrupt and final and comes with a sting you never quite get over.

An empty tomb was not enough, not for her.

The disciples, Jesus' twelve closest followers with a front-row seat for every miracle and private discussion with the teacher after every public address, spent resurrection morning locked in an upper room "for fear of the Jewish leaders."[2]

All of that private teaching hadn't amounted to much courage or perseverance, but it's hard to blame them. These twelve (actually, now eleven) men were well-acquainted with the harsh realities of this world and had only done a brief dance with hope, caught up in the story their renegade rabbi was weaving. They woke up like fools with hangovers. This morning, the effects have worn off and the realities of real life are slapping them in the face—the need for food, the need to explain, and most of all the need to get on with it.

They were hiding out together in a musty room with no food. They didn't have time to prepare. The whole thing had happened so fast. One minute they were walking off a Passover feast, and the next they were up all night at a trial that moved courtrooms several times before the death penalty was handed down. When they woke up on the hard floor, they were hungry.

They also had some explaining to do. That's where the fear comes in. Their rabbi had just gotten executed for blasphemy. Opposing the Jewish temple successfully feels fun and rebellious in the best kind of way when the priesthood is reeling, but when the priests ran to Rome with their robes tucked into their belts and the government bought their story, a heavy right hand landed very publicly on Jesus. Suddenly opposing the temple wasn't fashionably rebellious anymore; it was costly.

Then there was the confusion of how to square the cross with the three years that had gone before it. At least one of the disciples stood close enough to his cross to hear Jesus' raspy voice whispering prayers for the people driving the nails, the people mocking him, the ones spitting on his helpless body. "What kind of a manipulative spinmeister keeps up the act under those conditions?" They had to get on with it, but where does this leave them? What matters and what doesn't? Where do they go from here?

It's an ordinary Sunday, and an empty tomb isn't enough.

It's not enough to change everything they're facing.

It's not enough to lift the bounty they feel on their heads.

It's not enough to bring them out of that room into the light of day.

Jesus' disciples were realists, not gullible fanatics.

EMMAUS

A couple of Jesus' followers never even made it to the upper room. Two of them were halfway down the seven-mile walk to Emmaus, a village far enough from Jerusalem to start fresh but close enough to get to quickly on foot.

Luke's gospel paints a picture of these two, heavy with symbolism.[3] They are walking away from Jerusalem—the great city of faith, the setting of Jesus' ministry, the background of their spiritual formation. They are walking toward Emmaus. For ten chapters,[4] Luke's gospel is structured according to a journey to a city. Jesus "resolutely set out for Jerusalem,"[5] a redemptive journey toward the city. Two of his disillusioned disciples have traded that redemption journey for another. Their backs are turned to the city that symbolized all of their hope. They're making their way toward another city—a city of escape, a new start without the baggage, a consolation. They're trading in an enchanted sort of hope for something much safer.

Emmaus was a consolation prize. It was a walking declaration that "as it turns out, maybe life is much more harsh than hopeful, but I'll make the most of it while I can and making the most of it starts by getting some distance between myself and the hope I can live without as long as I don't have to be reminded of it."

This isn't a couple of unwavering dreamers looking for a reason to keep the faith; this is a couple of realists dealing with the death of their rabbi and, symbolically, the death of their hope.

THOMAS

Of all Jesus' followers, from those cloistered in an upper room to those hightailing it to Emmaus, Thomas is my favorite. He's always been my favorite.

The harsh realism of the other disciples was quickly turned upside down when Jesus started making supernatural appearances. It started with Mary Magdalene:

> Now Mary stood outside the tomb crying . . .
>
> They asked her, "Woman, why are you crying?"
>
> "They have taken my Lord away," she said, "and I don't know where they have put him."
>
> *John 20:11, 13*

Still a realist. Still thinking of potential grave-robbing suspects. What else could it be?

> At this, she turned around and saw Jesus standing there, but she did not realize that it was Jesus.
>
> He asked her, "Woman, why are you crying? Who is it you are looking for?"
>
> Thinking he was the gardener, she said, "Sir, if you have carried him away, tell me where you have put him, and I will get him."
>
> Jesus said to her, "Mary."
>
> She turned toward him and cried out in Aramaic, "Rabboni!" (which means "Teacher").
>
> *John 20:14–16*

The ten disciples (all who remained, except for Thomas) were next:

> On the evening of that first day of the week, when the disciples were together, with the doors locked for fear of the Jewish leaders . . .
>
> *John 20:19*

So now it's Sunday night, and they're still locked away in that room. The empty tomb doesn't have them piecing together the story of supernatural mystery. It has them locked up in terror. Faith in another world hasn't consumed them, but fear of this one has.

> Jesus came and stood among them and said, "Peace be with you!"
>
> *John 20:19*

Between those two appearances, Jesus had spent the afternoon walking to Emmaus. It took until the group of three stopped to eat for Jesus' two companions to recognize that they were speaking to the very man they knew to have died and been buried three days ago. Luke writes:

> When he was at the table with them, he took bread, gave thanks, broke it and began to give it to them. Then their eyes were opened and they recognized him, and he disappeared from their sight . . . They got up and returned at once to Jerusalem.
>
> *Luke 24:30–31, 33*

By late Sunday night, every living disciple has been greeted by a supernatural encounter with the resurrected Lord—except for Thomas. Mary Magdalene is frantically spilling out her story; the two followers from Emmaus are trying to catch their breath from a run in the dark so they can get theirs out; and the ten who witnessed his appearing are talking over each other, interrupting every couple of words, everyone wanting to deliver their version of witnessing a man walk through the wall of their locked room.

Thomas isn't entertained. Thomas isn't buying it.

Now Thomas (also known as Didymus), one of the Twelve, was not with the disciples when Jesus came. So the other disciples told him, "We have seen the Lord!"

But he said to them, "Unless I see the nail marks in his hands and put my finger where the nails were, and put my hand into his side, I will not believe."

John 20:24–25

In essence, he's saying, "I don't care if everyone else believes. If you're all so desperate to buy this, go ahead. If God wants me, he can come get me. I'm not hiding."

Beneath that blanket statement, there was something deeply personal. There always is. Always.

This is the moment Thomas is known for. It's the moment that defines his life for most, but a life defined by a single moment is always too small a picture. If you trace the story back, you'll see all that was behind his divine ultimatum.

THOMAS'S BACKSTORY

John 11 records the story of Jesus' return to Bethany. The last time Jesus was in Bethany, his life was threatened. He was promised a sure and brutal death if he dared to return. Naturally, all the disciples tried to talk him out of going—all of them except for Thomas, who said, "Let us also go, that we may die with him."[6] Jesus wanted to go back to Bethany, and Thomas was ready to go with him, even though he expected it would cost both of them their lives.

That is how completely Thomas hoped in Jesus. There's nowhere he won't go, nothing he won't give up. No sacrifice is too big. He is ready to die alongside his Lord if that's what it takes!

Then, just like that, the revolutionary leader was falsely accused, tried, and executed. The whole show was suddenly over.

Thomas was ready to die with Jesus. He wasn't ready to live without him. And when that fate, the one he wasn't ready for, was suddenly thrust on him, he learned a lesson we all pick up somewhere along the way: life is more disappointing than hopeful, so the safest way to live is to never get your hopes up.

Look at Jesus through the wounded, resurrection morning eyes of Thomas and realize that, for a moment at least, from his limited perspective it appeared that Jesus had spun a web. He had worked a great illusion. He had played on Thomas's needs and pulled on his hopes like the strings of a puppet and then, all of a sudden, had dropped him. Thomas must've been left wondering, *I guess it was all a hoax. I guess he was either a mentally ill deceiver or, at best, a well-intentioned madman, but it was a hoax, no matter how you spin it.*

Thomas was not a gullible fanatic; he was a realist. He was a realist who had gotten drawn into a big enough hope that when it appeared to fail him, he collapsed without the will to get back up. The world was seen through enchanted eyes for a time. God was living and active and all around him. Everything became brightly colored, and then he was asked to go on living without Jesus, and it all faded to black-and-white.

He was a strong-willed, fiercely logical realist. *Fine*, he thought. *If this world and my life in it is just the product of a wild accident or a Creator who designed it and then quickly lost interest, I can live with that. I can deal with a colorless world of unanswered questions. What I can't live with is someone trying to convince me that seeing in color is possible, that hope is alive. That wound is too fresh. That time was too real, that loss too great.*

ARZIMAT

Arzimat is one of the people who has been most formative in my own faith journey. He converted from Islam to follow Jesus in his early twenties, and in his family and culture, the cost was high. He was disowned by his father, kicked out of his home, cut off from his family of origin. Still, he remained convicted that his newfound faith was worth all that sacrifice.

A few years later, he was overseeing a parachurch ministry serving the Muslim community he had grown up in. Arzimat studied engineering and got a prestigious job offer from a high-end company straight out of school, and he walked away from all of it to serve the very community that had disowned him. Like Thomas, he willingly sacrificed his own dreams for the joy of (what he thought was) a better story. "Let us also go, that we may die with him."

He met Gulia, got married, and started a family of his own. Shortly into their marriage, she got pregnant—a boy—and all those parent-to-be excitements followed: phone calls to friends to share the news, talk of names, doctor appointments and sonograms as the anticipation built. She went into labor way earlier than expected, dangerously early—at just seven months. She rushed to the hospital and went through hours of agonizing labor. Finally, a stillbirth.

I can't imagine anything more painful. As a pastor, I've walked through miscarriages with so many grieving families as they ached from the loss. I've also celebrated new life in so many hospital rooms. But to go through the months of anticipation, the indescribable pain of labor, and then give birth to a tiny corpse? To never meet his eyes with your own, to never hear the sound of his crying voice, to never hold his body while a soul still lives in it—I can't imagine the pain.

Arzimat personally dug the grave for his firstborn. Because of his Christian faith, his home country would not allow his child a dignified burial in a cemetery, believing the curse of God to be the cause of death. We grieved with him. There are no words for the pain of digging a hole for the son you loved so deeply but never got to meet face-to-face. Arzimat was broken, but it was prayer that buoyed him through those waters.

A couple of years later, Gulia showed him a second positive pregnancy test—another son. The cycle started over—this time with the context of their pain. They mobilized so many of us to pray around the clock for health. They took extra precautions, extra doctor visits, extra care to ensure a healthy pregnancy. When the big day came, the birth was again premature—a couple months ahead of schedule. Of course they feared the worst. The hospital was flooded with praying people of faith who were full of hope, trust, and even joy.

Eventually, Arzimat stepped into the waiting room to make the announcement—another stillbirth. He had dreamed for two years of announcing the name of his little boy, of being hugged by friends who felt more like brothers and sisters, of crying tears of joy with a supernatural smile spread across his face. He wept in our arms, but it was tears of grief, not joy, on our faces.

He dug another grave. Same story. This time, with each cut of the shovel into the earth, saying, *I'm done. I'm done doing your PR, God. I'm done hoping and praying. What were you waiting for anyway? What combination of time spent praying and number of people praying and form of praying actually gets your atten-tion? What's the equation that awakens you from your apathy? For me, resurrection is a rumor I know nothing about. I've given you everything, and where were you when I really needed you? Where have you ever been when I've really needed you? I'm done.*

His story doesn't end there. He remains one of the most formative people in my faith journey, and today he is the father of three boys. That's a better ending, but it doesn't take away the pain in the middle—the pain of loss, the pain of confusion, the pain of screaming to the God you thought you knew and hearing only silence in return.

Maybe Arzimat's story is particularly dramatic, but the larger themes hold across every faith journey I've ever known, including my own. We are all Thomas.

As a student, I watched Bible college classmates show up as eighteen-year-olds so full of wonder that they were ready to spend decades telling the same story and never grow tired of it. But a look under the hood of the American church was so off-putting that they chalked up their own experience to emotionalism and manipulation during their more impressionable years and walked away from the story altogether.

As a New Yorker, I've watched people carry a sincere faith into a highly intellectual, culturally diverse, spiritually pluralistic city and find that the story they've been spoon-fed since childhood doesn't hold up against the complexity of the world they're actually living in.

As a pastor, I've watched people grow into their thirties and forties, faced with the realization that the life they had always assumed God wanted for them wasn't the life they were now living. *Reserving sexual intimacy for marriage made sense when I assumed I'd be married by twenty-five, but now I'm thirty-five and there are crickets on my online dating apps. Am I really gonna spend the rest of my life waiting on God to bring "the one" he's already a decade late on?*

I've watched people pray with hearts full of faith for healing and then watch their loved ones die.

I've listened to people recount debilitating abuse they faced as a child and ask, "How am I supposed to be healed now by the God who didn't rescue me then?"

I've prayed and counseled people of faith who have been crippled by mental illness for long stretches, and I've mourned when a few of them took their own lives. Where's the "renewing of the mind" we were promised?[7]

I've watched people get the life they wanted and be so disillusioned by it that they fall apart, and I've also watched people miss out on the life they wanted and be so disillusioned by it that they fall apart.

There are endless varieties to the plot, but no one gets through a life of faith without coming face-to-face with Thomas's disappointment in the days following resurrection. For all of us, he is our twin.

ISOLATION

Maybe you've already asked yourself the obvious question: "So if Thomas was one of Jesus' disciples, why didn't he encounter the resurrected Jesus when Jesus suddenly appeared in the upper room?"

That's what real, honest, existential doubt often does to us. It makes the community of belief nearly intolerable. Often, the first symptom of doubt is isolation. Like Thomas, we can deal with a black-and-white world, but we can't deal with a community of people trying to talk each other into seeing in color. In times of doubt, the human instinct is to withdraw into isolation.

When Jesus was in his spiritually darkest hour in Gethsemane, he wanted his three best friends right there with him. He didn't try to gut it out alone or grin and bear it. He invited his community into his pain:

> He took Peter, James and John along with him, and he began to be deeply distressed and troubled. "My soul is overwhelmed with sorrow to the point of death," he said to them. "Stay here and keep watch."
>
> *Mark 14:33–34*

We tend to do the opposite. When our souls are overwhelmed, the human temptation is self-isolation, to turn inward, not outward.

There's a strange comfort we find in withdrawing from a believing community during times of unbelief or uncertainty. Doubt can create the feeling that "I'm on the outside, and these people can't understand or relate." This feeling is almost always the product of perception, not conversation. It usually comes from looking at a whole group of people and categorically making assumptions about them, not the repeated experience of voicing our doubts humbly, honestly, and vulnerably to individuals in that community, only to have them be completely incapable of relating. Isolation happens when I assume, "The church will never accept me after my divorce. I can't bear the thought of sitting in the pew wondering what they're thinking." We make assumptions and push others away to protect ourselves.

The gut reaction of doubt is to withdraw. That's the instinct. It's the immediate comfort. The primary reason is that we need a bit of distance from a person or group representing belief in order to wholly dismiss them. Distance is dehumanizing. Haven't you noticed that it is much easier to invent narratives for the motives of a person or group when you don't have to look them in the eye and actually talk to them? Other people are much more easily dismissed when we can have dialogues with those other people only in our imaginations. So that's what we do. I've caught myself having an argument with someone in my subconscious mind in the shower, making points and counterpoints to what they'd say back, far more often than I actually have those conversations aloud.

And that's almost certainly what Thomas did. Where was he when Jesus showed up? I don't imagine he was on a bender, passed out in a brothel on some sketchy corner of Jerusalem's red-light district. I imagine he needed some space. Maybe he was alone, or maybe he went and found a few of his old friends at that spot where they used to meet up before he went all "Holy Roller" on them and joined the radical rabbi. Maybe he needed to sort things out on his own, or maybe he needed to say some things out loud that he didn't feel safe saying to Peter and John and the rest of them. I'm not sure. What I feel confident about is that Thomas needed enough distance from the other ten to convince himself that his experience was the true one, the honest one, the right one, the real one. He needed enough distance to dehumanize the experience of all the others.

There's another thing about doubt though. Agreement is affirming. A community of belief is so powerful when belief is strong within you. The upper room must have been a wonderful place to be after Jesus' appearance. Sharing a transcendent experience, reliving it through the shared experience of other witnesses, is almost as good as having the experience in the first place. But to walk into that upper room after a few days alone, sorting out the grief of your own spiritual setback and searching in silence without answers to honest questions—that can make that room a difficult one to tolerate.

Sometimes the truth is we aren't ready to seek reparations for our unbelief or fractured belief. Maybe the community surrounding us is actually making a lot of sense. Maybe we love and respect the people in it. Maybe we'd still like to laugh with them, make plans with them, or share meals with them, but we just can't stand to open up this subject with them because belief is a topic of pain or frustration or anger or just plain disinterest for us at the moment.

As understandable and human as that is, the funny thing about this brand of isolation is that we don't remain isolated for long. We still want the community belief used to give us— those people to share our experience and affirm us by under- standing and agreement, so when some believing community (be it a church, a group of friends, or something else) stops being the source of affirming agreement, we go looking for it somewhere else.

In times of doubt, we want to find people who agree with our doubts and affirm our version of skepticism. As a pastor, I've watched friends in the church over the years grow disappointed or skeptical (for completely understandable reasons), but instead of remaining in the believing community, sharing unbelief with the same candor that belief was shared with, the instinct is to withdraw, finding safety among others with a matching disappointment or skepticism.

That observation has become a source of sadness for me because building community around our doubt always feels comforting at first, but it's isolating in the end. It quickly delivers a sense of honest, loving, understanding camaraderie, but relationships built on a shared disagreement, a shared skepticism, and disenchantment can be paralyzing. It feels good to find other people who say, "Yeah, I feel that exact same way," but more often than not, these relationships do little more than give us the permission to sit down in our doubt—to stay in that place, to stop searching for answers and start changing the subject. Community that affirms you without challenging you will make you feel comfortable, but it will never move you, never heal you.

We all want to belong because we all want to be loved. We want to be known as we are and accepted as we are. The love of a community—any community—is great, but insufficient. No one, whether an individual or group, will ever offer us love so perfect that it never comes up against human limitations, never inflicts pain instead of love. We are made for a kind of love that always cares, always understands, and always remains, but that kind of love is only found in God. Life without community is incomplete; life with community but without God is bearable but tragically underwhelming and still incomplete.

Thomas was sophisticated in his disenchantment with God. His story was legit. The circumstances leading to his doubt were totally reasonable. He was ready to walk away from the "enchanted" and make the most of the story that would go on without any kind of ending worth living for. He was ready to just go on living, regardless if living carried the coherent meaning and purpose it used to, regardless if there really was any author with a pen in hand or not, even if he had to accept that this was nothing more than an improv show gone far off the plot without a director to recover it. Thomas was ready to swallow the hardest of pills, but he didn't. That's why I think walking back into the upper room on Sunday night might be the most courageous act found anywhere in the Gospels by someone not named Jesus.

DISAPPOINTMENT

Thomas has a nickname today; maybe you've heard it—Doubting Thomas. But I think it's the wrong nickname. I definitely don't think it's fair, but more importantly, I don't think it's accurate. Thomas spoke his doubt loud and clear in the face of belief:

> "Unless I see the nail marks in his hands and put my finger where the nails were, and put my hand into his side, I will not believe."
>
> *John 20:25*

But it wasn't doubt driving what he said; it was disappointment.

This is the full weight behind his words to the others on Sunday night in the upper room: "If the rest of you need to add a fairy-tale ending on top of a hoax that victimized every last one of us, be my guest. I get it. You're reeling. I am too. But I'm not gonna get through a lie by another lie. I'm gonna face the truth. Everyone and everything around me is dying. There is no transcendent meaning. There is no loving, personal, involved Creator. There is no hope. There is potential, and there is darkness, and the best this world's got is distraction. So I'm gonna learn to love the potential, even though it's shaded by darkness, and enjoy the distractions offered me in this life. If anyone ever again makes me think hard about the meaning of it all, I'll change the subject. I used to think that was a coward's way out, but with the hand I've been dealt, I think maybe it's the most courageous way through."

During the life of Jesus, Thomas's life was defined by hope. He didn't know where the story was going, but he was sure of this—he was living it with Jesus. Then the one thing happened he didn't expect, the one thing he never could've seen coming. Life ripped a rug out from under him, and he was flat on his back, and there, staring at the ceiling, he promised himself one thing: "When I muster up the strength to get back up on my feet, I'll never risk this kind of disappointment again. Whatever I have to believe, however I have to live, whatever I need to do to go on, I'll make sure I don't end up on my back like this ever again."

Thomas did get back up on his feet, and he kept moving forward, only now his life was defined by disappointment. The hope he had in Jesus—that was the foundation of everything for him before. The disappointment he was dealt by that hope—that was the new foundation. He was building a life on disappointment.

That's not just Thomas's story; it's our story—all of us. It's my story and it's yours, and if it's not yours yet, it will be soon enough.

Maybe, like Thomas, the foundation you're building on is a spiritual disappointment. *I walked out on the limb called faith with God once before, and it snapped underneath me and sent me tumbling helplessly to the ground. God turned out to be completely underwhelming, and the whole faith thing left me with a lot more pain to sort out than anything else.* If that, or some version of it, is your story, chances are your primary goal is to avoid getting hurt like that again by any kind of God or any kind of faith.

Nora

I was fidgeting for the right key in front of my apartment building when I saw her pretend not to see me. "Nora!" I greeted her more excited than I really was. I was holding two massive Ikea bags full of laundry, feeling like my arms were right on the verge of tearing out of their sockets. She looked up at me and tucked her hair behind her ear, and I could see the track marks where tears had stained her face.

That's why she tried to keep her head down and walk by, I thought. "Nora, what's going on?" She had attended the church I pastor for years, but we had only ever shared a handful of conversations. It was mainly casual greetings and occasional small talk.

It was her sister. She had just gotten off the phone with her. She was suicidal—one failed attempt already—and Nora was the only one she'd told. We stopped everything and prayed through tears right there on the busy sidewalk, my laundry on either side of us. Her countenance changed as we prayed. Nothing objective had shifted, but you don't make it into your thirties with a practiced faith intact in a city like New York unless it's substantive—and her faith certainly is. She believed all those stunning promises of Jesus about prayer—ask, seek, knock; if you remain in me, ask anything you wish; if you believe, you will receive whatever you ask for.[8] Her despair was repurposed into hope as we laid it before God together.

That was the first of many such prayers. Every time we talked in the coming months, the news about her sister grew worse. She was bipolar-depressive and battling a narcotics addiction. She was done with psych meds, done with rehabs, done with God. She had tried it all and she had dug a pit, she thought, that was too deep for anyone or anything to reach into to pull her out.

Eventually, Nora couldn't bear the emotional roller coaster of praying and waiting on a God who seemed absent (at best) and unforgivably apathetic (at worst). I stopped seeing her face among the sea of faces most Sundays. She didn't throw her faith out altogether, but God had disappointed her deeply enough, personally enough, that it became difficult to bear the company of the blissfully believing. They were like her that crisp night praying next to those bags of laundry—hopeful.

Nothing is as isolating as hope when, for you, it's a fairy-tale rumor. *Maybe I can bear adjusting my expectations for a God who overstated himself, but to surround myself with people who haven't felt that branch snap, haven't felt the free fall that hope leaves us all in sooner or later—that's too much.* So Nora reluctantly distanced herself.

Her story isn't over, and my vantage point is limited. But it saddens me that in her collision with sobering disenchantment, the church didn't seem a safe, dignifying place to rediscover the hope she was suddenly living without.

Larry King

Maybe it's something else, like your career. *I thought in some undefined place in my gut that if I broke into this industry or got this job title or worked my way to an offer from this company, I'd be someone, but then I finally got it. And it turns out, I'm still me—problems, insecurities, discontentment, and all.* That realization will rock you. It will lay you on your back. If that—some version of it anyway—is your story, chances are the life you turned to in consolation is a living reaction to that disappointment.

■ ■ ■

I watched an interview of a veteran broadcaster that got my attention. It was a coronation. He had just received a lung cancer diagnosis that at his age looked fatal. So Larry King, typically the interviewer, sat down as the subject of a candid interview looking back on a historic career.

Inspiring doesn't do it justice. He has an incredible story of working his way up from the bottom to become arguably the most successful television reporter of all time.

Then the interviewer took a sharp turn into King's personal life, asking about his family. He has been married eight times to seven different women. At the time of this writing, he has five children, nine grandchildren, and four great-grandchildren—and by his own admission almost no relationship with any of them.

"I just never figured marriage out. Being a father didn't come naturally. My career was my marriage. My career was my parenting." That was the gist of his response, redirecting back to his professional accomplishment quickly and seamlessly.

All of the inspiration I had felt turned to sorrow.

This man who had become so much was obviously ending his life so empty. He was reaching his end, and all he'd accumulated in this life he couldn't take with him. He won the game he was playing and, in the process, lost everything he couldn't get back.

Thomas Merton wrote empathetically, "If I had a message to my contemporaries, I said, it is surely this: Be anything you like, be madmen, drunks, and bastards of every shape and form, but at all costs avoid one thing: success . . . If you are too obsessed with success, you will forget to live. If you have learned only how to be a success, your life has probably been wasted."[9] There are a thousand cautionary tales telling us it's empty at the top, that whatever you have to sacrifice on the climb isn't worth it and you'll never get it back. Still, we can't seem to resist finding out for ourselves.

Ray

Perhaps for you it is a relationship. *I have longed for "the one" for so long. I have hoped so completely for a deep sense of companionship with another human being, and all that waiting has just compounded into more waiting. So today the risk of another disappointment is less bearable than just accepting a life of relative loneliness.* If some version of this is your story, chances are the hope of potential human intimacy is now a terrifying threat of debilitating disappointment.

▪ ▪ ▪

I was sitting on the ratty couch in my tiny Manhattan apartment. It was 1:00 a.m.—late enough for something uncharacteristically honest to spill out of him.

The backstory is important. Ray's parents were good people, but uninterested agnostics. No real interest in God. Certainly no interest in church. Their only strong conviction was that everyone who thought they had the answers couldn't be trusted.

A friend invited him to something called "youth group," and Ray liked it. It was different in a good way, not what he expected. A few months in, his heart was profoundly captured by Jesus.

There I am, sitting on a ratty couch across from that kid, now in his thirties, and the faith that seemed unbreakable then is now hanging by a thread. He explained. "My experience is that God is present so long as your life plays out according to the evangelical script—married by twenty-six, 2.5 kids, stable job, predictable journey. Church is kind to you when your life unfolds on schedule. But when your story doesn't match that story, church feels like an awkward fit for you, like you're still hanging around a crowd that moved on without telling you. And you get tired of asking God the same questions and listening to the same silence."

He was zeroing in on a cold truth he had never articulated before, not even to himself. "I guess it's this simple for me: I fell for a God I was told was knocking on the door of my heart, and I'm just not sure I can believe that anymore."

Whatever lies at the core for you, we all know what it is to live defined by disappointment. Every last one of us does it at some point, and most of us do it forever.

THE TWIN

Several hundred years after Thomas's death, the moniker "Doubting Thomas" stuck, but he lived by another nickname before that one. More formally, his Greek name was Didymus, but the disciples called him by the Aramaic translation— Thomas. Both names translate as "the twin." The Twin—that's the original nickname, which is perfect . . . because in a way, he's the twin of all of us.

Plenty of us could say right along with Thomas, *It's not enough. An empty tomb is not enough.* But as you join your voice to his, you owe it to yourself to also ask, *What's the personal version of that statement for me? What disappointment defines my experience?*

Friedrich Nietzsche wrote of hope, "In truth, it is the most evil of evils because it prolongs a man's torment."[10]

We are much quicker to see the world through disappointment than hope because it's safer. Building our lives on disappointment won't make anything better, but it will protect us. It will cover us like fig leaves and keep the most vulnerable parts of us hidden. When we are mentored by our disappointment, we get uneasy around hope; we learn to resist it at all costs. Allowing disappointment to play a defining role in your life might guard you from pain, but it will also most definitely guard you from any greater hope that might bring life.

The stuck place Thomas finds himself in is a familiar one to all of us. Peter James Cameron paints the picture:

Each of us lives with the unextinguishable expectation that life is supposed to make sense and satisfy us deeply. Even the most jaded atheist feels cheated if he doesn't experience meaning, purpose, peace—in a word—happiness in this life. But just where does this universal expectation for personal fulfillment come from? It isn't something we drum up or manufacture on our own. Rather, the burning yearning for "what is real" is incorporated into our design. This burning can lead either to the torment of pain or the torrent of love. It will either consume us or consummate us.[11]

Thomas couldn't bring himself to believe in resurrection, but he also couldn't keep himself from believing in, and fighting for, life—and life to the full.

CHAPTER FIFTEEN

BUT SOME DOUBTED

Now Thomas (also known as Didymus),
one of the Twelve, was not with the disciples
when Jesus came. So the other disciples
told him, "We have seen the Lord!"
    But he said to them, "Unless I see
the nail marks in his hands and put my
finger where the nails were, and put my
hand into his side, I will not believe."
John 20:24–25

I thought I recognized him lying there in a pack of homeless men. It was difficult to say for sure, because he had one hand on a cell phone more beat-up than Edward Norton at the end of *Fight Club* and the other hand shading his eyes. He was bundled in layer on top of layer (the way you do if you're planning to spend an entire February sleeping outside), but there was a kid—a teenage boy—among the men. And I think I know him.

ANDRES

Some backstory will be helpful: I was barely twenty-two years old when I moved to New York City. My first apartment was rodent-infested, barely insulated, and smelled constantly like the restroom of a dive bar. Everyone who has ever moved to

New York without an Ivy League degree (and maybe even with one) has a story like that.

I founded and led a weekly youth ministry serving at-risk youth in the Lower East Side, home to North America's most densely populated block of government subsidized, low-income housing.[1] I met Rainey through that ministry. She is brave in that way that seems almost accidental. She takes risks that seem to never strike her as risks, but rather as the only logical step. She's compelling in that humble way you want to be around. She's laid-back and fun, and she laughs hard and often. But she's also fiercely committed to living what she believes. That's why she, a single woman in her mid-twenties living on a public school teacher's salary, legally adopted Andres.

Dre was a boy in Rainey's eighth-grade class. He missed enough days to be expelled. He slept with his head on his desk most of the days when he did show up. Most teachers would dismiss him as a lost cause. But he had Rainey for third period, and where most people pull back, she pushes in. As it turned out, Dre had been abandoned by the one, single parent he knew. He wasn't sure if he had any other family to turn to, and he had somehow slipped through the foster care system's fingers. He was living homeless in Tompkins Square Park—in the eighth grade.

Eventually, he was picked up by the police and sent to a juvenile detention center a couple of hours' drive out of the city. He was charged with illegally sleeping on a park bench in a New York City park. Rainey was watching all this play out, and that's when she decided to begin the legal adoption process.

The process was long and painful but always hopeful. In the end, the judge granted her a trial-period adoption with plenty of conditions, and Dre moved into the spare bedroom she had set up in her tiny Chinatown apartment.

It takes a village, right? So Rainey assembled one, and I was a part of it. Kirsten and I had a standing weekly dinner at Rainey and Dre's place, and I spent Thursday afternoons with him solo. He had stories that made your jaw drop, and others that made your heart heavy. But in every way, he was a normal kid. He had a crush on a girl, and he really, really wanted to make the high school basketball team. We added Tuesday morning basketball drills to our weekly hangouts—6:00 a.m. at the Chinatown YMCA (he was an early riser, still on the incarceration routine).

Everything was going according to plan. Dre was going to school, passing his classes, and honoring his parole. He was surrounded by love and support. Rainey had given away her whole life, and it wasn't for a cause or a systemic problem; it was for this one, single kid. It was breathtaking.

Then he ran away.

"Tyler, are you with Dre? He hasn't come home." Rainey had called me, looking for him. One ordinary day after school, Dre never came home. There were no warning signs, no withdrawal. He was just gone. The police found his parole-issued ankle bracelet (used for tracking his location) somehow broken off and removed. Several days went by so slowly that it was almost unbearable. Then, about ninety-six hours after disappearing, he just showed up at Rainey's place.

When "the prodigal son" comes back home with his tail tucked between his legs, the Father forgives him without an explanation and throws the kind of party you talk about for weeks. We decided this model was worth following. Rainey gathered Dre's "village," and we killed the fattened calf, which, if you live in Manhattan, means we let Dre choose the restaurant.

"I've always wanted to eat at Olive Garden."

"Really? You know we're on an island that renowned chefs come to from all over the world, and we're giving you free pick to go anywhere, right?"

"I've always wanted to eat at Olive Garden."

That's how we ended up at a table on 23rd Street with bottomless breadsticks.

It was the kind of night you'd never forget. Ragamuffin holiness—the way I imagine it felt to have dinner with Jesus. We had the time of our lives, but we could also feel the weight of something truly transcendent hanging over our table.

Not long after that night, Dre was gone again.

Didn't come home from school. Picked up by the cops. No second chances this time. Out of Rainey's legal custody. Property of New York State. Out of the bottom bunk in Rainey's tiny spare bedroom and back to the bottom bunk of a cell in that familiar juvenile detention center. I never got to see him again. Never got to understand. Never got to say goodbye.

Fast-forward about three years. There's a kid—a teenage boy—lying among the men. And I think I know him. It's Dre. A patchy, scraggly beard covers pieces of his boyish face, but it's Dre. I'm in Tompkins Square Park—the park with a global reputation for heroin in the heart of Alphabet City, where he used to sleep at night as an eighth grader.

I walk over. "Dre, is that you?"

"Yo! What's up, Ty?"

"What are you doing here, man? Are you out of juvy? Are you okay? Are you hungry?"

The last question is the only one he answered. He ate a couple of pepperoni slices faster than I've ever seen anyone do it while I peppered him with questions. He was eighteen now, homeless, sleeping on that familiar park bench—the only place that really felt like home. His company was a group of homeless addicts two or three times his age. I offered him my apartment, a couch to sleep on, a shower, even a spare key. He didn't want any of it. He was happy to see me, but he didn't want my help.

DOUBT

I can still remember exactly how it felt to walk home that day. With very little effort, I'm walking those routine steps across Tompkins Square Park, taking in the familiar, signature scent of dog poop and weed and who knows what else blending in the air. People are passing me everywhere, but I'm staring straight ahead, looking right through every last one of them into the hazy, gray winter afternoon.

For once, I didn't have anyone listening to my prayer. No need to clean it up or make it come to a resolution in the end for the congregation. I was mumbling to God—being honest about the facts, not forcing them into my tidy little framework.

"Why, God?"

"How, God?"

"Are you there, God?"

"Because if you are, you've got a lot of explaining to do on this one. He's just a kid. How could you watch this happen?"

It's one thing to lob impersonal accusations at God from a safe distance, like, "What kind of God would stand by while the Holocaust happened?" It's another thing entirely for those accusations to become so personal that they intrude into your world, crashing into your rib cage with such force that they put you on your back. That's what doubt feels like. Typically, doubt doesn't feel like an existential question posed by your philosophy professor, a question your local pastor has an underwhelming answer for.

Doubt is an experience in the world you can't reconcile with the story you believe.

And that is exactly what was happening to me—the pastor on his day off, suddenly suffocated by doubt.

Doubt is not, *I've got a few questions I'm gonna need to have satisfactorily ironed out before I can commit to this set of ideas.*

Doubt is, *Why, God? How dare you, God? Are you even there, God? And even if you are there, if this is how you run things, do I even care to know you, God?*

"Tyler? What are you doing?" It was Kirsten. I was standing in front of our apartment door, hand in my pocket, gripping my keys but not moving. I wasn't even sure how long I'd been there.

"I just had a slice of pizza with Dre." I don't remember what I said after that. It wasn't anywhere near coherent. Not yet anyway.

DOUBT: THE CHURCH'S GREATEST FEAR

The church of our day gets pretty nervous around doubt.

Remember what Thomas said?

> "Unless I see the nail marks in his hands and put my finger where the nails were, and put my hand into his side, I will not believe."
>
> *John 20:25*

That's how Thomas responded to the resurrection rumor that his closest friends excitedly shared with him. I wonder how this response would fly in most of our churches. I've attended more church services than I can count and sat in who knows how many church-based small groups, and I can count on one hand the number of times I've heard doubt addressed head-on or heard anyone voice doubt among the believing. But I've heard story after story of those riddled with silent doubt who were unable to find the space to bring it into the open, until one day they walked out the door and took the doubt conversation somewhere other than the church.

I've heard every confession under the sun. There's almost nothing that can surprise me a decade into pastoring New

Yorkers. I pastor a church in one of the most post-Christian environments on the globe, where a spirituality that survives the city is often (falsely) viewed as a victory for Christians. Still, even here, I've heard doubt confessed just three times in my conscious memory. Three times. In ten years.

I wonder if our communities have the space available to be as honest as Thomas was. I wonder if we honor one another and trust God enough to let the question fill the air without puncturing a gut-level question with an oversimplified, head-level response. I wonder if the Bible makes more room for God to meet people in the midst of doubt than the communities that are formed around the very same Bible.

Most importantly, what do we make of a God who (spoiler alert) met Thomas in the midst of doubt? This is a God who wasn't offended by this doubt but who drew near, making his presence known in the midst of doubt, responding to Thomas's honest rant like it was an invitation.

One of the Bible's most famous passages is found at the very end of Matthew's gospel. The Great Commission is a favorite, go-to passage for most preachers. The vast majority of church-goers will have heard it enough to recite it (or get close).

The resurrected Jesus gathers his disciples one more time on the Mount of Olives. He's a master leader creating a moment. Bringing them back to that familiar place where they've shared so many defining moments. The Messiah meeting his ragtag band of followers in the location sure to drag back up to the surface the full context of their individual stories: the hope and the pain, the miracles and the disappointments, the triumphs and the failures—all of it. Then when the weight of the moment is almost buckling every knee, he says it:

"All authority in heaven and on earth has been given to me. Therefore go and make disciples of all nations, baptizing them in the name of the Father and of the Son and of the Holy Spirit, and teaching them to obey everything I have commanded you. And surely I am with you always, to the very end of the age."

Matthew 28:18–20

The King hands off the keys to the everlasting kingdom to his apprentices. What a moment! But of all the times I've heard this passage talked about, and all the different preachers I've heard explain it, every single time, without fail, they've conveniently sidestepped a pretty crucial line that immediately precedes those famous words:

Then the eleven disciples went to Galilee, to the mountain where Jesus had told them to go. When they saw him, they worshiped him; but some doubted.

Matthew 28:16–17

But.
Some.
Doubted.
And to a group that included some men and women full of belief and hope and others riddled with doubt and uncertainty, Jesus says, "Here's my name, reputation, power, and kingdom. It's yours to give to the world now."

What does it tell us about the heart of God that he put the keys to the kingdom in the shaky hands of people who were something less than certain? That he looks the doubter in the eye and says, "Not at some future point when you get every intellectual quibble sorted and every question answered, but right in the midst of your doubt, I choose you. I trust you. I send you."

Apparently, Jesus was much more comfortable with doubt than most of our churches are.

BELIEF: THE CULTURE'S GREATEST FEAR

But if the church is afraid of doubt, our post-Christian culture is at least equally afraid of belief. After all, doubt is so much more fashionable than belief. Doubt is thought inherently intelligent, thoughtful, and respectable, while belief is usually lumped in with categories like narrow-minded, gullible, and inconsiderate.

Philosopher and professor Dallas Willard put it this way:

> We live in a culture that has, for centuries now, cultivated the idea that the *skeptical* person is always smarter than the one who believes. You can be almost as stupid as a cabbage, as long as you *doubt*. The fashion of the age has identified mental sharpness with a pose, not with genuine intellectual method and character.[2]

It is worth considering the thought that belief is more inherent to human beings than doubt. We are all born believers. You've never met a skeptical toddler who is grappling with emotional angst. You came into this world with a readiness to believe, a relentless kind of hope, a free self-giving love, and a heart bent toward justice. What biblical scholars call the *imago Dei* ("image of God") was alive in you at first. Cynicism and skepticism, to whatever extent we carry them, were picked up somewhere along the way in this world.

It's what the psychologist George Sargent called "learned meaninglessness." He recounted his own therapist, who said, "George, you must realize that the world is a joke. There is no justice, everything is random. Only when you realize this will you understand how silly it is to take yourself seriously. There is no grand purpose in the universe. It just *is*. There's no particular meaning in what decision you make today about how to act."[3]

The modern person is schizophrenic when it comes to belief

and doubt. We want belief (we always have), but we also fear disappointment. "We are simultaneously both cynical and gullible," writes Pete Greig, "fearful of missing out yet afraid of commitment too."[4] We want deep meaning, but we want it packaged in a way that protects us from pain. We want true love without ever risking rejection. The battle between belief and doubt is often the intellectual expression of a deeper emotional battle between love and fear.

New York Times op-ed columnist David Brooks wrote an article a few years ago that got my attention. He was exploring a trend in the modern generation of young adults—that being cold and detached have become fashionable. Today, disenchantment is admired. We (I say "we" because I am a part of the young adult generation he describes) are always investigating but never committing, suspicious of commitment, and especially suspicious of anyone who dares to be committed. The premise of the article is a generation of people with educated opinions but fearful lives, unwilling to walk out on any limb of committed belief because they're fearful it will snap beneath them. Near the close of the article, Brooks offers these observations:

> We are all fragile when we don't know what our purpose is, when we haven't thrown ourselves with abandon into a social role, when we haven't committed ourselves to certain people, when we feel like a swimmer in an ocean with no edge.
>
> If you really want people to be tough, make them idealistic for some cause, make them tender for some other person, make them committed to some worldview that puts today's temporary pain in the context of a larger hope.
>
> Emotional fragility seems like a psychological problem, but it has only a philosophical answer. People are really tough only after they have taken a leap of faith for some truth or mission or love. Once they've done that, they can withstand a lot.

We live in an age when it's considered sophisticated to be disenchanted. But people who are enchanted are the real tough cookies.[5]

There was a time in history when belief was so common that the courageous move—the really dangerous leap—was to doubt. Today, cynicism, skepticism, disenchantment, and uncertainty are so common and doubt has become so fashionable that maybe the tables have turned. The most honest, most courageous, most reckless move is belief.

There was a time in history when people were tempted to doubt. Could it be that people today might be tempted to believe?

TEMPTED TO BELIEVE

Even if belief is tugging like a temptation at our culture, we still need encounter with the living God. We need a moment of clarity when it all makes sense, when I find my individual story overlapping with the great resurrection story. We need a collision point of stories.

Because if you think Thomas was a tough sell, just take a look in the mirror.

Malcolm Gladwell was a guest on Oprah Winfrey's podcast, and after about a half hour of responding to her questions, he posed one to her: "One question I have always wondered about is: What does it mean to change someone's mind?"[6] Let me try to rephrase that question in a more robust way: What conditions would have to be true for you to hear something and have it change your life forever?

In 1975, Stanford University conducted a study to explore what it takes to change the mind of an individual who is already set on a conclusion. The test involved suicide notes.

Each undergraduate student was given a pair of suicide

notes—one real note provided by the Los Angeles coroner's office, and one fake note produced by the conductors of the study. The students' task was to distinguish between the real note and the fake one. After collecting the results, some students were told they nailed it, choosing correctly 96 percent of the time. Another group of students was told they had quite a bit of trouble, choosing correctly on only 10 percent of the notes.

What the students were told was all just part of the setup though.

At this point, the surveyors revealed the truth: The score that had been awarded each person was entirely fabricated. They had gone through that entire portion of the exercise simply to tell them they had a knack for discerning the truth or shouldn't trust their instinct and then tell them, "Never mind. We lied about that part. No one has actually learned anything about suicide or about themselves so far today. We've simply wasted your time up to this point."

Now this is where it gets interesting.

The students were then asked to guess their own accuracy, to estimate their ability to discern the truth. In an article in *The New Yorker*, Elizabeth Kolbert wrote:

> The students in the high-score group said that they thought they had, in fact, done quite well—significantly better than the average student—even though, as they'd just been told, they had zero grounds for believing this. Conversely, those who'd been assigned to the low-score group said that they thought they had done significantly worse than the average student—a conclusion that was equally unfounded.[7]

People didn't change their minds about what they believed, even when the facts their beliefs were based on were proved entirely false. Fascinating!

Like good scientists, the Stanford professors overseeing

the study needed to be sure their conclusions would hold over multiple experiments and a broader range of test subjects. So they waited until the opportune time and set the hook again.

A few years later, they assembled a similar study involving two firefighters and followed this pattern: Students were given false information and were allowed to form conclusions based on complete fiction. Then the moderators revealed the deception, calling the whole thing a hoax and explaining that the students had spent all that time learning absolutely nothing true. Again, this is where it got interesting. The students continued to trust the false information gained from what they were unequivocally told was a false test.

The conclusion was simple. In the words of the researchers, "Once formed, impressions are remarkably perseverant." Said a bit more clearly by another researcher, even after the basis "for their beliefs has been totally refuted, people fail to make appropriate revisions in those beliefs."[8]

People don't change their minds about what they believe, even when their belief is proven to be entirely illogical. There must be something more than logic wrapped into our beliefs. There must be some emotional attachment, some piece of human identity we fear losing by changing our minds. You see, it's really, really hard to move someone from a belief (including the belief that no one has any real idea what's worth believing in).

Stanford couldn't help themselves. They went back for more evidence—or maybe just to mess with undergrads again. You can decide for yourself on that.

This time around, researchers surveyed students in advance, intentionally selecting students with opposing views on capital punishment—50 percent were in favor of it and thought it minimized crime, while the other 50 percent opposed it and believed it to have no consequential effect on crime.

The students were given two identical studies. One provided compelling evidence for capital punishment; the other made an equally compelling case for the other side. Both studies were fake. You really can't trust these Stanford professors, can you? The studies were filled with false statements of fact and fabricated evidence dreamed up by the researchers to provide an airtight, convincing case for each side. At the end of the experiment, the students were again asked about their views. Not only did no one change sides; the two views moved even further apart. The *New Yorker* article reveals, "Those who'd started out pro-capital punishment were now even more in favor of it; those who'd opposed it were even more hostile."[9]

Human beings have a remarkable ability to ignore evidence that contradicts their beliefs and an equally remarkable ability to exaggerate evidence that confirms their beliefs. People don't change their minds. They guard and protect their conclusions. Any evidence that might call our current belief systems into question is unconsciously identified as an attack by the human brain and fended off by any means necessary.

I think it's probably worth reminding ourselves at this point that these people who seemed so easily deceived, so stubborn, so unwilling to move from a factually false belief were very intelligent people. This wasn't a collection of America's Most Gullible. It wasn't even a group selected at random. This was a collection of magna cum laude, top-of-their-class valedictorians who were then studying at Stanford and are now your boss's boss. These were well-read, fiercely logical people.

How many readers of this book got into Stanford? I'd guess none because if you got into Stanford, you'd be way too busy reading tons of other books. Regardless of your background, culture, experiences, SAT score, IQ, Myers-Briggs type, Enneagram number, or job title, once you've made up your mind, you're probably not moving.

There are plenty more studies and books written about the nature of human rationale and how we arrive at our conclusions (or, more accurately, our convictions), so I won't belabor the point except to say something you already know simply by being honest with yourself: facts don't change our minds, much less our lives.

So that brings us back to the original question: What conditions would have to be true for you to hear something and have it change your life forever?

Because while we may be stubborn and hard to convince, every life has moments like that in it. We can look back across our years and see moments where information came in and we walked out forever different.

Sometimes it's personally tragic news—a medical diagnosis, the death (or maybe suicide?) of a loved one, a national or global event that particularly rattles us. Sometimes it's personally wonderful news—your wedding day, a positive pregnancy test, an acceptance letter, a winning lottery ticket, the lead role in the play you auditioned for. Other times it's a "first"—first breakup, first layoff from a job, first outright rejection. There are moments where the conditions are such that "my life will never be the same."

But life is mostly not those moments. Life is mostly ordinary, humdrum moments, uneventful days, and focus on making it to the weekend. In the flow of ordinary life, void of drastic interruption, most of us are not actually open to change. We have settled into our ways of thinking, our ways of doing, our basic assumptions about the world. We are comfortable there. It would take a lot to move us.

If we are emotionally set on an explanation that makes sense of the world, we can take in plenty of factual evidence contradicting that story, but we will easily deflect it, usually without any serious consideration. We effortlessly dismiss facts that don't confirm our predetermined conclusion. We are wired this way for self-protection. Staying put, even if we are living on a false foundation, feels safer than moving. That's the fact that outweighs all the others.

What conditions would have to be true for you to hear something and have it change your life forever?

I'm a pastor, and that means (among other things) that one day out of every seven, I stand in front of a room filled with people and talk about the biggest questions every last one of us faces but spend the vast majority of our lives distracted from really considering. One thing I always hold in my mind—maybe the one thing that keeps this weekly routine from ever really feeling routine—is this: the bravest person in the room is the one trying to figure out if I've got anything meaningful to offer at all or if I'm a complete quack who decided way too early in life on set conclusions to the questions that really matter, and now I'm stuck mumbling nonsense to a mostly bored audience.

The bravest person in any church on any Sunday is the person honestly trying to figure out if Jesus is worth real consideration, because if he is, it will probably mean questioning the foundation their entire life is built on. It means the conclusions that have always made them feel safe aren't safe anymore. The bravest person in the rows of flimsy, white Ikea chairs set out in the old Jewish synagogue we rent to hold church in each Sunday is the undecided person who is honest enough to ask the questions that matter.

The most courageous person holding this book is the one with a healthy combination of skepticism about the author and sincerity about the search for answers.

So this brings us back, one more time, to a question worth real consideration: What conditions would have to be true for you to hear something and have it change your life forever?

It's not evidence. We are changed by *encounter*—the overlap of objective and subjective information. Information I've found easy to overlook plenty of times before is now colliding with my personal story at just the right moment in just the right way. *That's* what changes us.

CHAPTER SIXTEEN

MY LORD AND
MY GOD

August 1974, New York City

In August 1974, the World Trade Center, already known as the Twin Towers, was having the finishing touches put on before the financial center of the world flooded the 104 prestigious floors of high-status office space. After months of planning, training, and traveling back and forth between New York and France, Philippe Petit snuck into one of the towers just before closing time, took the stairs to one of the highest floors (still a construction site), hid for hours huddled under a tarp to avoid security guards and cameras, and then snuck up to the rooftop. After rigging up a tightrope as the sun rose, a man spent about a half hour dancing on a wire between Manhattan's new skyline icons.

For the first few minutes, nobody noticed. But then when the first couple of people spotted him, clusters started to gather. It's Lower Manhattan—the financial center of the globe—so when the world's most serious and powerful businesspeople have stopped their frenetic dash into the office to stare at the sky, people notice. A crowd quickly gathered. The extremely busy, overscheduled people rushing into work to move the world's money around for a few hours . . . stopped. The whole city stopped for a half hour that morning, wondering at the spectacle in the air.

© New York Post / Shutterstock

This is the most famous photo from that day. It wasn't famous the day it was taken. Actually, it took nearly thirty years for it to become consequential at all, but it became iconic for obvious reasons today: a plane passes in the sky behind this man, and from the depth perception of this photo, it looks eerily low and much too close.

Two moments are captured that caused everyone in New York City to stop and wonder—the whimsy of a man dancing between the towers and the tragedy of a plane colliding with those same towers. Two events, thirty years apart, accidentally caught in the frame of a single photo.

The stories overlapped for just a moment.

LET THE GREAT WORLD SPIN

Colum McCann's novel *Let the Great World Spin* tells five stories of New Yorkers: an Irish immigrant trying to scratch out a life in the city; a young, wealthy couple in the West Village;

mother and daughter prostitutes in the Bronx housing projects; the wealthy wife of a successful judge on Park Avenue; and an elderly African American woman, twice divorced, who lost all three of her sons in Vietnam. It traces the changing circumstances of these five as they move through life stages and unique challenges. Though the characters and their stories are fictional, the book keeps resetting to a true event. Each chapter starts over again on August 7, 1974, when a man walked across a wire between the Twin Towers.

Honestly, it was a series of good stories for a while. I was definitely entertained by it and even recommended it to a friend when I was only halfway through.

But when I opened to the final chapter, when all these very different stories collided in the climactic scene, I read with tears behind my eyes. There's just something about the collision point of stories—the overlap. It's a beautiful mess.

McCann writes, "A man high in the air while a plane disappears, it seems, into the edge of the building. One small scrap of history meeting a larger one. As if the walking man were somehow anticipating what would come later. The intrusion of time and history. The collision point of stories."[1]

And now we're back where we started—the collision point of stories; the moment when distant stories overlap in a single frame. That's the encounter.

EARLY FIRST-CENTURY JERUSALEM

On an otherwise ordinary morning in Roman-occupied, first-century Jerusalem, an event happened that equally caused everyone to stop and wonder.

Less than seventy-two hours before, the body of Jesus of Nazareth, a rural revivalist preacher with the apparent power to heal and claims of messianic fulfillment had been quieted once and for all, tucked safely away in an airtight cave donated at the last moment by a man offering to cover the burial expenses.

Early one morning, in the midst of the day-after-the-Sabbath rush hour, word started to circulate that the tomb was empty. Royalty and peasants, soldiers and civilians, Roman rulers and Jewish priests, oppressed and oppressor—not a single person escaped the wonder of the moment when the tomb was mysteriously empty. It stopped the whole world. And the reason the whole world is still talking about this one event on that otherwise ordinary morning is that it is a moment frozen in time, like a photo capturing three stories in a single frame:

1. The Story of the World
2. The Story of Jesus
3. The Story of Our Twin (Thomas)

A Week Later

A week later his disciples were in the house again, and Thomas was with them. Though the doors were locked, Jesus came and stood among them and said, "Peace be with you!" Then he said to Thomas, "Put your finger here; see my hands. Reach out your hand and put it into my side. Stop doubting and believe."

Thomas said to him, "My Lord and my God!"

John 20:26–28

The first phrase of this passage is the one that gets me. "A week later . . ." What is Jesus waiting for? Other translations give a more precise figure: "eight days later . . ."[2] So if Thomas was honest enough, both with himself and with his friends, to name his spiritual doubt and personal disappointment, and if God responded by meeting Thomas and delivering just the kind of "scabs and scars" proof he was looking for, why wait a week? After all, Jesus is in a resurrected, heavenly body walking through walls and making supernatural appearances seemingly on a whim, so it stands to reason that this particular appearance would have been more prompt.

What is Jesus waiting for?

For the collision point, for that moment when the three great stories overlap in the perception of this one man: the story of the world, the story of Jesus, and the story of an individual life—in this case, Thomas.

In her book *When the Heart Waits*, Sue Monk Kidd tells the story of a conversation she had with a monk.

> Later I sought him out. "I saw you today sitting beneath the tree—just sitting there so still. How is it that you can wait so patiently in the moment. I can't seem to get used to the idea of doing nothing."
>
> He broke into a wonderful grin. "Well, there's the problem right there, young lady. You've bought into the cultural myth that when you're waiting you're doing nothing."
>
> Then he took his hands and placed them on my shoulders, peered straight into my eyes and said, "I hope you'll hear what I'm about to tell you. I hope you'll hear it all the way down to your toes. When you're waiting, you're *not* doing nothing. You're doing the most important something there is. You're allowing your soul to grow up. If you can't be still and wait, you can't become what God created you to be."[3]

"MY LORD AND MY GOD!"

Eight days after resurrection morning, Jesus appeared to Thomas. He showed up in the same upper room, just as he had before, but turned specifically to the Twin and said something like, "Here. Run your fingers over the scabs on my wrists. Touch the wound on my side. Now believe! You have died a silent, internal death in the face of your disappointment. Here's a way to live again!"

That was the collision point. That was the moment Jesus waited eight days for. That was when Thomas saw "the story of the world, the story of Jesus, and the story of his one individual life" all in a single frame. His feet were standing on earthly soil, well-acquainted with the potential and limitations of this life. He had walked the distance of the story of Jesus, experiencing life as it was meant to be lived and the horrific injustice of death, and now resurrection was moving from fairy-tale theory to something tempting enough to wake up his dormant hope.

But the moment all this clicked is so personal. God saw the whole world spinning mad, but he also saw Thomas's world spinning mad. He climbed down, right into the place of Thomas's personal brand of pain and disappointment, his particular need, and said, "Here's a way to live again!" Anthony Bloom writes, "A relationship becomes personal and real the moment you begin to single out a person from the crowd."[4]

That's exactly what Jesus did on resurrection morning in the garden when he went from a general explanation to a personal address: "Mary."[5]

It's what happened when Jesus showed up on the shore and called out to Peter, "Throw your nets on the other side!"[6]

And it's what Jesus did in an upstairs hideout in central Jerusalem when he held out his scarred wrists to Thomas, saying without words, "This is what you were waiting on, right? I haven't given up on you, Thomas. Don't you give up on me."

Jesus revealed himself in the way Thomas needed to know him, and, sure, Thomas could've explained that away as a lack of sleep or groupthink or something like that. He could've let fear win, played it safe, and kept his guard up against any future disappointment, but this wasn't an empty tomb he was looking at—it was the presence of the living God.

Met by God's living presence, the words tumbled effortlessly from Thomas's mouth: "My Lord and my God!"[7] Lost in the translation is the power of this declaration. Scholars call it the highest praise given to Jesus anywhere in the four Gospels. No one ever thought more of God than Thomas did when God showed up in the place of his disillusionment, pain, disappointment, and doubt. Frederick Buechner writes:

> Unless we see with our own eyes, we will not believe because we cannot believe, cannot believe fully anyway, cannot believe in a sense that affects the way we live our lives . . . If men [and women] are to believe in his resurrection in a way that really matters, they must somehow see him for themselves . . . Now as then, it is not his absence from the empty tomb that convinces men [and women], but the shadow at least of his presence in their empty lives.[8]

An empty tomb was never enough. Not for anyone. It never has been and never will be. So what are we looking for? The presence of the living God. It is not a better explanation of Jesus that the world waits on, but the experience of his living presence.

God reveals himself in the collision point of stories. He finds us trapped between two unsatisfying stories, getting through days by changing the subject, learning to cover ourselves with fig leaves one disappointment at a time, and says, "Here's a way to live again."

A STORY WORTH TELLING

The HBO series *True Detective* had its ups and downs, but the climactic scene to season 3 was a magnum opus. The pieces of the case were clicking into place for the lead detective (played by Mahershala Ali). The voice of his wife (played by Carmen Ejogo) narrates:

> "What if the ending isn't really the ending at all? . . . What if there's another story? What if something went unbroken? All this life, all this loss, what if it was really one long story that just kept going and going until it healed itself? Wouldn't that be a story worth telling? Wouldn't that be a story worth hearing?"[9]

I believe something *did* go unbroken.

I believe there is one big story, and it *does* end in healing—and so your story can too.

I believe there *is* a story worth telling—a story worth hearing.

Two Kinds of Problems

Resurrection is about terminal problems. Before it's a polarizing story of a real-life superhero, it's a common story we all know too well—death. The opening scene doesn't feature a triumphant God-hero; it features a few women carrying burial spices to the tomb, the ancient Near Eastern equivalent of placing flowers on a grave. The scene essentially opens at the viewing that precedes a memorial service. "I'm so sorry for your loss. Is there anything we can do?"

A supernatural resurrection may seem a million miles away, but the abrupt ending we call death? That's the air everyone was breathing on resurrection morning, and that's a scene you don't have to think about too hard to find yourself in.

Death is a rude, unwelcome interruption, and grief is like a sickness we just have to ride out until it passes—if it passes. While we've constructed a way of living that lets us pass the vast majority of days without asking the most important questions, death storms in abruptly, kicks down our door, robs us of that illusion, and leaves the living behind to ask the questions they used to blissfully ignore.

No matter who you are, how you look, what you do, where you live, or how important you are in a particular room . . . you are going to die. No matter how good you get at ignoring your death and pretending life goes on forever . . . you are going to die.

Are you taking anything with you? Is there anything, anything at all in your life, that the looming death awaiting you isn't going to snatch like a thief?

"Is there anything I have that death cannot take?" This is the question we asked in chapter 4. Death is the great scale that weighs out the worth of everything we are and everything we do. And death is a terminal problem.

Resurrection is about internal problems. In *Straight Pepper Diet*, the brutally honest memoir of Joseph Naus, the author describes the best day of his life. Joseph was around twelve years old, staying over at his best friend Collin's house. They went to the movies, ordered pizza, and made root beer floats, and on Saturday morning, the whole family gathered around a pancake breakfast. Collin's mom later drove Joseph home.

Well, *home* is the word he used for it. It was actually a fake house he had picked out for the pretend life he told everyone he had. She drove Joseph "home" that Saturday morning, to that fake house where she'd dropped him off so many times before. Joseph would walk to the front door, wait for her Mercedes sedan to pull away, and then walk about a half mile to his real home. Only this time, when Collin's mom pulled up, there was another family playing in the front yard of his fake house.

She sat in the driver's seat silently for a moment, letting the realization land on her, unlearning something she had taken as fact. It was only about five seconds, but it felt longer. It was long enough for tears to build up against the dam of Joseph's eyelids.

"Where do you *really* live?" she asked.

He lived in the nearby housing projects with a single mom who was a low-functioning addict. Their building was situated right on the edge of a school zone, so he went to school with suburbanites with two-parent homes, a dog, cash to spend on movies, and Saturday pancake breakfasts.

He pretended not to hear her. "Thanks for the movies . . . for letting me spend the night . . . and the pizza." And he scrambled out of the car before she could see his tears.

Joseph writes these words about himself: "As he walked away, he thought of how he would never see her again and that he would never sleep over at Collin's again, not after what had just happened, not now that she knew."[10]

The instinct to hide in order to protect ourselves—to hide our weakness, our emotion, to never be really, fully seen—it's the most ancient instinct. The forbidden fruit was tasted; a world made perfect was corrupted; and Adam hid from God. He held back his tears, shielded his emotion, and hid his weakness. He sewed fig leaves together and walked out like nothing happened.

Eventually, Adam walked out of the Garden of Eden, thinking of all that had been lost, thinking he would never really be seen by God again—"not after what had just happened, not now that [God] knew."

We all have our own unique cocktail of what counselors call "presenting issues"—resentment, fear, loneliness. None of us live apart from our expression of the universal condition, but we all have an endless itch to hide it from anyone who gets close enough to see.

The famous philosopher Søren Kierkegaard defined the biblical concept of "sin" not as the breaking of moral rules but as "before God . . . not to will to be oneself."[11] Sin is not wanting to be yourself before God. The biblical story isn't an outdated fairy tale. It's your story and mine. It's the cosmic story and the most personal story at the same time.

There are two kinds of problems that are universal to every human being:

1. The *terminal* problem: nothing lasts past the death awaiting us.
2. The *internal* problem: we all live with struggles that we try to numb or hide.

What are the possible solutions to that equation?

One is to simply resign yourself to the fact that you can't do anything about it, so you may as well live for the moment as much as you can. Get as much as you can for yourself before it's gone, and do whatever you need to do to deal with the pain in the meantime.

But . . .

"What if there's another story? What if something went unbroken? All this life, all this loss, what if it was really one long story that just kept going and going until it healed itself? Wouldn't that be a story worth telling? Wouldn't that be a story worth hearing?"

What if this death isn't the end after all? What if there's a God who took the period off the end of the sentence and let this thing go on forever?

And what if this God can fill your life and heal your resentments, fears, and loneliness in such a profound way that you'd actually want to live forever because you'd finally be whole?

RESURRECTION

One of the things that distinguishes Christianity from other faith movements is that it traces its origin to a definitive event. This isn't true for Judaism, Buddhism, Islam, or atheism. This event is called resurrection.

Everyone deals with the terminal and internal problems, and the solution for every other belief system is a philosophy—an enlightened state to transcend human problems. Jesus stands out because he didn't teach a solution; he *became* a solution. The word for that is *resurrection*. You don't have to take Jesus' solution, but you do have to face these two problems either way, and that makes his story worth hearing at the very least.

Resurrection Is about Death

Resurrection looked like a funeral at first because God was dealing with the terminal problem of the human race—the one no one can escape. When Jesus walked out of a grave, he was essentially saying to anyone willing to listen, "The end doesn't have to be the end. There's a kind of living that's unbroken by death. There *is* something death cannot take."

Resurrection Is about Shame

Resurrection deals with the hiddenness we inherited and never grow out of. It allows us a "naked and unashamed" way of living again.

I carry a coin with me everywhere I go. It's a three-year sobriety chip from Alcoholics Anonymous. It was given to me by Miles. He said some nice words about our community's role in his battle with addiction and told me he wanted me to have it. So every day since, it goes with me everywhere.

Miles also invited me to join him for a meeting—to see the other community that has shaped and supported and freed him.

I sat in a metal folding chair in the back row of a church basement on 6th Avenue in the West Village. The meeting opened with a celebration of the people recording their first thirty days of sobriety. One by one they stood, identified themselves, and received a light, slightly bored round of applause.

"Hi, I'm Steve, and I'm an alcoholic. Eleven days." Light applause.

"I'm James, and I'm an alcoholic. Twenty-three days." Light applause.

"Glen. Alcoholic. Seventeen days." Light applause.

It went on like that a few more times. And then this kid in his early twenties stood up, shaky and visibly nervous. Through a quivering voice he forgot (or skipped) the familiar lines everyone else recited and barely got it out through the emotion: "One day."

No one flinched. There was no applause. A silence hung in the air while this young man stood above everyone else in all his vulnerability.

Metal chair legs screeched against the old tile floor on the other side of the room as an elderly man (I later found out he had more than thirty years of sobriety under his belt) stood up and began to climb over the rows of occupied chairs in front of him. He didn't shimmy out to the aisle. He just swam through everyone in the way until he got to this kid, who had now begun to sob, and hugged him. He just stood there holding him for a long time, while the whole room broke into the loudest roar of applause I've ever heard in a church basement.

What makes you do that? What makes you climb out of your seat, hurdle several rows in your old age, and embrace a total stranger? What makes you risk embarrassing yourself for the new guy?

Because it's one thing to hear that a guy's fighting his demons and trying to get sober. That's the general story. But it's another thing to know what it feels like to spend a night in the drunk tank, to go out for a couple of beers and wake up on a sidewalk, to vomit on your desk at work, to urinate on your own bedroom carpet, to ruin your marriage, to disappoint your kids, to hurt everyone you love the most, and to accidentally trade everything you have of real value for something so cheap.

How bad does it have to get for a twenty-three-year-old to stand in a room of strangers and say, "I need help. And it's day one"?

That elderly man knew exactly how bad. He understood that shame. He had lived it.

Resurrection is this also. It's God's way of swimming across all the neat rows of chairs to embrace everyone who will honestly let themselves be seen by him. Because there's not a moment of the pain he hasn't lived right beside you. Because he knows exactly how bad it's been.

Resurrection is about shame because it brings it to an end. It turns hiddenness into a lie and nakedness into coming alive.

What if there's a better story than shame?

What if there's healing so complete that there's nothing left to hide?

Resurrection Is about Victory

Gospel isn't an inherently Christian word; it's the English translation of the ancient Greek word *euangelion*, common in the early centuries, meaning "good news." Set in its original Roman context, the image it may provoke is that of a soldier astride a horse, riding through the narrow streets of Rome, calling loudly, "*Roma Victrix!*" to any who would hear. An announcement of military victory—"good news."

Alongside that common image, the Christian gospel provokes a comical parallel. A poor beggar runs through the same streets, shouting out through a hysterical smile, "*Christus Victor! Christus Victor! Christus Victor!*" to any who have the audacity to believe. Resurrection is not a theory or philosophy; it's gospel, a declaration of victory, an announcement of astounding news, a full-throated exultation of a decisive triumph in behalf of the human race.

We all have terminal and internal problems we can't solve.

In resurrection, Jesus is victorious over those very things. That victory is then made personal, to be pressed down into the individual human heart.

Because of this victory, Jesus takes on himself the consequences of your presenting issues, dysfunction, and failed attempts at self-sufficiency; all the mistakes you've made; and the horrible brokenness you've been an innocent victim of. In exchange, he gives you the consequences of his perfect righteousness—restored relationship with God, a perfect view of the self, and a unique participatory role in the story of ongoing redemption.

The gospel is not a formula for getting on God's good side; the gospel is the news that everything you need for salvation and abundant life has already been accomplished fully, finally on your behalf. *Christus Victor!* Jesus sums it up in his final words: "It is finished."[12]

You don't sacrifice everything unless you believe the reward is worth it. The gospel is God's declaration that you are his reward, and you are worth it.

Resurrection Is about Us

The biblical story doesn't end with God whisking off a lucky few into a utopia in the sky. That's a rumor that started with Plato and accidentally stuck in certain branches of the church, but it has nothing to do with Jesus.

Jesus talks constantly about bringing heaven to earth, not getting people to heaven. His mission is not to get you into heaven; it's to get heaven into you. Read every single recorded sermon in Acts, and you'll notice a pattern: Not a single one focuses on salvation as a way to escape the fires of hell and book a room in a much more preferable location in the sky. Instead, the good news is always about eternity invading this life. The end of the story isn't a pious few strolling the golden streets in the clouds.

The final pages of Revelation picture heaven coming to earth—the whole world redeemed, renewed to its original purpose as a paradise of unbroken communion between Creator and creation.

When Thomas uttered, "My Lord and my God," he wasn't booking a future reservation at an ideal endpoint. He wasn't entering a supernatural waiting room where he'd hide out until his name is called. He was receiving resurrection life then and there. He was becoming the eternal, redeemed kind of life right in the midst of this fallen world. In the resurrection story, heaven is something that happens within us before it happens around us. Heaven is held internally before we one day see it externally.

Dallas Willard calls this "the extended incarnational plan."[13] Luke 10 records an occasion when Jesus sent out seventy-two of his followers to act by his power and authority, preparing for his arrival in the towns and villages on their shared mission. When they returned, joyfully celebrating the effectiveness of their ministry, it was at this point that Jesus saw the darkness retreating and the light growing:

"I saw Satan fall like lightning from heaven."

Luke 10:18

Let me translate this: When God shared his power with common people, the darkness of this world was drained of power. Divine power sharing with unqualified people is the way redemption grows. The fall came through human hands, and redemption is passed through human hands.

Resurrection is an invitation to a finished work on our behalf, but it's also a unique, participatory role in ongoing redemption. An invitation to breathe in the very life of God, to begin living a redeemed life right here and now, and to join in filling the earth with that very life until it covers every square inch.

To say yes to Jesus isn't to sign up for a reserved spot in the clouds behind the pearly gates; it is to join in the family of the redeemed, to collectively become a living preview of the promised future. William Willimon writes:

> The most eloquent testimony to the reality of the resurrection is not an empty tomb or well-orchestrated pageant on Easter Sunday, but rather a group of people whose life together is so radically different, so completely changed from the way the world builds community, that there can be no explanation other than that something decisive has happened in history.[14]

Resurrection Is about You

The way Jesus spent his fifty days on earth in a supernatural, resurrected body tells us everything we need to know about the heart of God. It would stand to reason that Jesus would make the biggest splash possible—appearing in Herod's palace or Pilate's courtroom or the Roman Colosseum. But you won't find Jesus in any of those places. Instead, he appeared, one by one, to each of his doubting, disillusioned, disappointed followers, calling them by name and restoring their belief. He hasn't offered us an empty tomb, but his living presence here, now, among us, with us.

Resurrection is for the whole world! And yet it's also for you. It's the broadest story and the most personal story.

What I'm getting at is this: *you are in the resurrection story*, like it or not.

This is what suddenly hits you in the presence of the living God. The biblical story is not one potential theory to explain this life; it's the story of every individual life, which means the resurrection is more than just a first-century Jewish legend. It's a current invitation to fully, finally come alive.

We all snatch the pen from the Author's hand. We all replace God, choosing the self for the center. And when we do, we interact with the same themes in our own unique ways, attempting to cope in the space between unfathomable potential and recurring darkness.

There's something in us that says "changing the subject" can't be enough. The something in us is a *longing for true life.* There's something in us that rises up to fight for a world that is better and more whole—it's a *longing for a truer home.*

The invitation offered by the resurrection is a very personal one—hope alive again, new life breathed into your lungs, resurrection in you! Resurrection happened so that resurrection happens.

In an interview, describing her own encounter with God, Anne Lamott described her newfound faith: "So I swear, IT WAS AN ACCIDENT!"[15] That's more or less how it always happens. A relational encounter with the living God. Lamott doesn't describe a long, intentional spiritual search that resulted in finding God; she describes a slog through life on her own terms, until one day she stopped changing the subject, and that's when she was found by the God she had been avoiding. She didn't go searching for love; love came after her.

Thomas wasn't convinced by the evidence of an empty tomb. But when he asked, he met the presence of the living God. Have you tried asking?

HOLY SATURDAY

Travis, my younger brother, was born less than seventy-two hours before Teddy, my paternal grandfather, died. My dad welcomed the birth of his son and then very quickly drove four hours across state lines to be with his siblings who were gathered around his father's deathbed. They were taking turns staying overnight in the hospital so someone would be with him at all times. It was my father's turn the night Teddy's heart stopped beating.

The following night, Dad was in the car again, driving four hours back home to be with his three-day-old newborn son.

I think about that drive often. This was a world before cell phones and podcasts. This was the world of radio or silence. Those were the only two options for solo road trips. He chose silence. He drove for four hours, suspended in silence between death and life—remembering and grieving death, anticipating and looking forward to new life.

One Saturday night as I stared blankly at an ironing board, I was thinking of my dad's drive, how he stared blankly out onto the highway underneath a clear, starry sky. I was ironing the wrinkles out of my only white dress shirt, and I was doing a terrible job of it. I only iron once a year, and tonight was the night. That level of infrequency means that each time I turned the shirt over, I discovered I had ironed new creases into the other side. How do some people make this look so effortless? While I was running the iron over the creases I had somehow made worse, I was wondering how visible the slightly yellowed stains under the arms would be to someone who got stuck with a front-row seat if I happened to get a bit too carried away with hand gestures.

It's Saturday night. For most of my thirty-some years on this earth, Saturday night has meant friends, food, laughter, and, most important of all, a few hours of complete freedom from the loom of responsibility that hangs constantly over adult life. Then I became a pastor. Among other things, my Saturday nights would be very different from now on. While everyone else is in peak-weekend freedom, I'm cramming for tomorrow's sermon. Being a pastor sometimes feels like having a big presentation due to the whole company first thing on Monday morning, every Monday morning. My "Monday" just happens to be called "Sunday," and the company is a congregation.

And this isn't just any Saturday night; it's Holy Saturday. The Saturday night just before Easter Sunday. The annual "iron the white shirt" Saturday night.

HOLY SATURDAY

The Bible is full of three-day stories.

When Abraham goes to sacrifice Isaac, he finds the ram caught in the thicket on the third day.

Joseph's brothers are released from prison on the third day.

Rahab hides the Israelite spies and was promised safety on the third day.

Esther fasts for her people and goes in to see the king on the third day.[1]

The pattern can also be found in the prophecies of the Old Testament and the letters of the New Testament, but you get the point. The Bible is a book of three-day stories.

Here's the big one: Jesus died on Friday and was resurrected on Sunday, which begs the question, "Why is there a Saturday?" A day of death and a day of life, sure. But why a day of silence in between? Why isn't every three-day story a two-day story?

Here's my theory: because our whole lives happen on Saturday.

Our whole lives happen in the silent space between death and new life. All of our waiting, hoping, disappointment, pain, doubt, and faith—it all happens on Saturday. We are all my father on that silent road trip, suspended between death and new life.

Sunday had come and gone, but Thomas was stuck on Saturday. New life was here! But he was still suspended in that place of waiting between death and life.

Maybe you're stuck on Saturday too, living in the space between death and resurrection. For those who want to keep living on Saturday, even after Sunday has arrived, God usually lets them. If you prefer to keep God at arm's length, locked away in a cage of theory that never risks relationship, God usually gives you what you want. He rarely will overwhelm people with his presence who aren't looking for him at all.

Real spirituality begins, though, when a person stops theorizing about God and begins actually attempting to know God. That's how it's always worked. Theory is safe and predictable because you get to remain in control. Theory happens on your terms. Relationship, on the other hand, is anything but safe and predictable. Relationship is to surrender control, to be open to disappointment again, but maybe, just maybe, on the other side of an attempt to actually know God, you'll find life. Maybe the voice that calms your restlessness and the peace that stills your anxiety are found in the very risk you can hardly stomach taking—the risk of relationship with God.

Thomas brought all of his pain to God, and God took the invitation to encounter. He has a better story than jaded disbelief, the safety of cynicism, and a crowd of comforting, like-minded disenchantment for one reason alone: He had the audacity to tell God exactly what he thought. He didn't dilute his theories. He didn't filter the pain of his past or the anger and the disappointment of his present. He brought all of it directly to God, and the most surprising thing happened—God responded.

We have more in common with history's famous skeptic than we care to admit most of the time, but his life can also be a guide to walk with, a real-life picture to awaken our hope.

Be really honest with yourself: Is this resurrection life the foundation you're building on as your numbered days roll by? Maybe, just maybe, as you're reading this, something is colliding for you—that great collision point of stories—and to your utter surprise, the words are almost coming out involuntarily. You can feel the whisper under your breath: "My Lord and my God."

ACKNOWLEDGMENTS

For the last two years, nearly everything I've written down or said publicly has been first uttered in conversation with my very good friend Caleb Clardy. Caleb pastors a sister church in Brooklyn (Trinity Grace Church Park Slope), and he and I work very closely together. I respect his creativity, integrity, and life as much as anyone I've ever known.

All of the ideas read in this book cannot be separated from him. His creativity is so tightly intertwined with mine that I can't parse out where each thought began, so with his permission, I offer that caveat. Whoever reads this book and is helped by it in any way—it is due to Caleb's imagination and humility.

Thank you to my friends who helped get these words into print. In particular, Simon Morris and Matt Hanner patiently combed through multiple drafts. Their fingerprints are all over this thing.

Thank you to my colaborers, whose insights are peppered throughout these pages. Pete Hughes, Darren Rouanzoin, John Mark Comer, Jon Tyson, Mark Sayers, and many others are the real minds behind this book. I'm just a clever thief.

Thank you to my team at Oaks Church Brooklyn:

- Alessandra—for living by risk and obedience always
- Sam—for believing in me and reminding me of who I am
- MJ—for putting up with me and trusting me
- Carlos—for fighting to know me beneath my role

- Megumi—for refusing to let me take myself too seriously
- Patrick—for warning me about the dangers of acronyms
- Gemma—for loyalty, for daily standing by me, shoulder to shoulder, and holding the weight of the church

Thank you to my family—Wils, Beck, Trav, and Josh. I have you to thank for everything. Josh, you, in particular, have cut a path for me to walk behind my whole life.

NOTES

Chapter One: *Stuck between Two Unsatisfying Stories*

1. Viktor Frankl, *Man's Search for Meaning: An Introduction to Logotherapy* (Boston: Beacon, 1992), 125.
2. Henri Nouwen, *Making All Things New: An Invitation to the Spiritual Life* (San Francisco: Harper & Row, 1981), 28–30.
3. John 10:10.

Chapter Two: *Unfathomable Potential*

1. See Jan Wong, *Red China Blues: My Long March from Mao to Now* (New York: Anchor, 1996), 277–78; see also Kris Cheng, "Declassified: Chinese Official Said at Least 10,000 Civilians Died in 1989 Tiananmen Massacre, Documents Show," *Hong Kong Free Press*, December 21, 2017, https://hongkongfp.com /2017/12/21/declassified-chinese-official-said-least-10000 -civilians-died-1989-tiananmen-massacre-documents-show.

Chapter Three: *Recurring Darkness*

1. John Ortberg, *Eternity Is Now in Session: A Radical Rediscovery of What Jesus Really Taught about Salvation, Eternity, and Getting to the Good Place* (Carol Stream, IL: Tyndale, 2018), 39.
2. G. K. Chesterton, *The Everlasting Man* (London: Hodder & Stoughton, 1930), 60.
3. Theodore Dalrymple, *Not with a Bang but a Whimper: The Politics and Culture of Decline* (Chicago: Ivan R. Dee, 2008), 83.
4. Karl Rahner, *Servants of the Lord* (New York: Herder and Herder, 1968), 152.

5. C. S. Lewis, *The Problem of Pain* (1944; repr., New York: HarperCollins, 2001), 70.

6. This idea is inspired by Johannes Hartl's *Heart Fire: Adventuring into a Life of Prayer* (Edinburgh: Muddy Pearl, 2018).

7. This definition of sin was first articulated to me by Caleb Clardy. I share it here with his permission.

8. Richard Dawkins, *The Selfish Gene* (Oxford: Oxford University Press, 1989).

9. David G. Benner, *Soulful Spirituality: Becoming Fully Alive and Deeply Human* (Grand Rapids: Brazos, 2011), 135.

10. Tara Westover, *Educated: A Memoir* (New York: Random House, 2018), 199.

11. David Foster Wallace, "This Is Water," https://jamesclear .com/great-speeches/this-is-water-by-david-foster-wallace. This speech was originally published on the Kenyon College website, http://bulletin-archive.kenyon.edu/x4280.html.

12. Russell D. Moore, *Tempted and Tried: Temptation and the Triumph of Christ* (Wheaton, IL: Crossway, 2011), 20–21.

13. Monsignor Lorenzo Albacete, "Adoration Vigil for Holy Thursday Night," in *Magnificat* 17, no. 1 (Holy Week 2015): 125.

14. See Ezekiel 47:1–12.

15. Quoted in Terre Spencer, "It's Hard to Get Enough of What *Almost* Works," www.jungatlanta.com/articles/summer11 -hungry-ghosts.pdf.

16. Gilbert K. Chesterton, *Orthodoxy* (New York: Lane, 1908), 24.

17. Marilynne Robinson, *Gilead: A Novel* (New York: Picador, 2004), 208.

18. Viktor Frankl, *Man's Search for Meaning: An Introduction to Logotherapy* (New York: Pocket, 1963), 363.

Chapter Four: Abrupt Ending

1. "Assisted Living Statistics: A Deeper Dive into the Demographics," American Senior Communities, February 23, 2016, www.asccare.com/assisted-living-statistics-a-deeper-dive -into-the-demographics.

2. "Where Do Americans Die?" Stanford School of Medicine, Palliative Care, https://palliative.stanford.edu/home-hospice -home-care-of-the-dying-patient/where-do-americans-die.

3. Ernest Becker, *The Denial of Death* (New York: Free Press, 1973), 17.

4. Matthew O'Reilly, "Am I Dying? The Honest Answer," TED, July 2014, www.ted.com/talks/matthew_o_reilly_am_i_dying _the_honest_answer?language=en.

5. Leo Tolstoy, *A Confession* (Mineola, NY: Dover, 2005), 21.

6. See Nola Taylor Redd, "It's Official: The Universe Is Dying Slowly," *Scientific American*, August 11, 2015, www.scientific american.com/article/it-s-official-the-universe-is-dying-slowly.

7. Becker, *Denial of Death*, 12.

8. Luc Ferry, *A Brief History of Thought: A Philosophical Guide to Living* (New York: HarperCollins, 2011), 261.

Chapter Five: An Ordinary Tuesday Afternoon

1. Luke 12:25.

2. See Francis Spufford, *Unapologetic: Why, Despite Everything, Christianity Can Still Make Surprising Emotional Sense* (New York: HarperCollins, 2013), 7–8.

3. John Ortberg, *Who Is This Man? The Unpredictable Impact of the Inescapable Jesus* (Grand Rapids: Zondervan, 2012), 187.

4. Richard John Neuhaus, *American Babylon: Notes of a Christian Exile* (New York: Basic, 2009), 161–62.

5. Jean Paul Sartre, *Essays in Aesthetics* (New York: Philosophical Library/Open Road, 2012), 1.

6. Julian Barnes, *Nothing to be Frightened Of* (Toronto: Vintage Canada, 2008), 1.

Chapter Six: A Way to Live

1. 1 Corinthians 15:45.

Chapter Seven: God: The Scandal of Abba

1. Barbara Brown Taylor, *Leaving Church: A Memoir of Faith* (San Francisco: HarperSanFrancisco, 2006), 147–48.

2. Genesis 17:1. The NIV text reads, "God Almighty"; the NIV text note reads, "*El-Shaddai*."

3. See Exodus 3:1–22.

4. Exodus 20:7 KJV and NIV.

5. Joachim Jeremias, *The Prayers of Jesus* (London: SCM, 1967), 57.

6. In the Babylonian Talmud (Mas. Chagigah 15a), the Holy Spirit is depicted in Genesis 1:2 as moving over the face of the waters "like a dove," a sign of messianic anointing and a symbol of what was to come through this man's life.

7. Matthew 3:17.

8. A. W. Tozer, *The Knowledge of the Holy* (1961; repr., San Francisco: HarperSanFrancisco, 1992), 1.

9. Abraham Joshua Heschel, *Man's Quest for God* (Santa Fe, NM: Aurora, 1998), 5.

10. This idea is explored in Frederick Buechner, *Telling Secrets* (San Francisco: HarperSanFrancisco, 1991).

11. Nancy Mairs, *Ordinary Time: Cycles in Marriage, Faith, and Renewal* (Boston: Beacon, 1993), 54.

Chapter Eight: Self: The Trouble with Fig Leaves

1. Eugene Peterson, *Run with the Horses: The Quest for Life at Its Best* (Downers Grove, IL: InterVarsity, 1983), 38.

2. Matthew 12:49–50.

3. See Luke 15:11–31.

4. I find that many writers attribute these words to Dickens, but I can't find a direct quote. It seems likely Dickens said this orally, making it more a probably true legend than a quote that can be traced to one of his writings. It's referenced by a number of authors (including John MacArthur in *A Tale of Two Sons*), and it can be found all over the web.

5. Timothy Keller, *The Prodigal God: Recovering the Heart of the Christian Faith* (New York: Dutton, 2008).

6. A. W. Tozer, *The Knowledge of the Holy* (1961; repr., San Francisco: HarperSanFrancisco, 1992), 1.

7. C. S. Lewis, *The Weight of Glory: And Other Addresses* (1949; repr., New York: HarperOne, 2001), 38.

8. Frederick Buechner, *Telling Secrets* (San Francisco: HarperSan Francisco, 1991), 44–45.

9. Søren Kierkegaard, *Papers and Journals: A Selection* (London: Penguin, 1996), 295.

10. Mary Karr, *Lit: A Memoir* (New York: HarperCollins, 2009), 384.

Chapter Nine: Others: Lepers, Prostitutes, and Tax Collectors

1. Fyodor Dostoyevsky, *The Brothers Karamazov: A Novel in Four Parts with Epilogue* (New York: Farrar, Straus and Giroux, 1990), 57.

2. Dostoyevsky, *Brothers Karamazov*, 58.

3. Genesis 3:12.

4. See Leviticus 14:1–32.

5. Matthew 8:2.

6. See Leviticus 13:45.

7. Gregory Boyle, *Barking to the Choir: The Power of Radical Kinship* (New York: Simon & Schuster, 2017), 166.

8. John Ortberg, *Who Is This Man? The Unpredictable Impact of the Inescapable Jesus* (Grand Rapids: Zondervan, 2012), 75.

9. M. Tullius Cicero, "For Plancius" 15, in *The Orations of Marcus Tullius Cicero*, trans. C. D. Yonge (London: Bell, 1891), www.perseus.tufts.edu/hopper/text?doc=Cic.%20Planc.%2015&lang=original.

10. Mark 2:14.

11. Mark 2:17.

12. Thomas Kelly, *A Testament of Devotion* (1941; repr., New York: HarperCollins, 1996), 81.

13. Brennan Manning, *The Ragamuffin Gospel* (Colorado Springs: Multnomah, 2015), 38.

14. Ortberg, *Who Is This Man?* 82.

15. Zadie Smith, *White Teeth* (New York: Vintage, 2000), 49.

16. Robert Bellah et al., *Habits of the Heart: Individualism and Commitment in American Life* (Berkeley: University of California Press, 1985), 72–73.

17. Matthew 5:48.

18. Luke 6:36.
19. Gene Knudsen Hoffman, "The Compassionate Listening
    Project," www.compassionatelistening.org.
20. 1 John 4:16.

Chapter Ten: World: A Curse Soaked into the Soil
1. Luke 7:11.
2. Luke 7:13.
3. Luke 7:14.
4. Matthew 14:13–21; Mark 6:32–44; Luke 9:10–17; John 6:1–13.
5. See Mark 1:32–34; Matthew 4:23.
6. See Mark 4:35–41; Matthew 8:23–27.
7. See John 11:38–44.

Chapter Eleven: Recovering the Plot
1. E. M. Forster, *Aspects of the Novel: The Timeless Classic on
   Novel Writing* (New York: Harcourt, 1927), 86; see Frederick
   Buechner, *Telling Secrets* (San Francisco: HarperSanFrancisco,
   1991), 1–2.
2. Buechner, *Telling Secrets*, 2.
3. Luke 4:18.
4. See Philippians 2:6–8.
5. Richard J. Foster, *Prayer: Finding the Heart's True Home* (San
   Francisco: HarperSanFrancisco, 1992), 61.

Chapter Twelve: A Way to Die
1. John Ortberg, *Who Is This Man? The Unpredictable Impact of
   the Inescapable Jesus* (Grand Rapids: Zondervan, 2012), 164.
2. Clayborne Carson, ed., *The Autobiography of Martin Luther
   King, Jr.* (New York: Grand Central, 2001).
3. Henri J. M. Nouwen, *Life of the Beloved: Spiritual Living in a
   Secular World* (New York: Crossroad, 1992), 118.
4. Ronald Rolheiser, *Sacred Fire: A Vision for a Deeper Human
   and Christian Maturity* (New York: Image, 2014), 285–86.
5. Rolheiser, *Sacred Fire*, 286.

6. Mark 15:39.
7. Pete Greig, *How to Pray: A Simple Guide for Normal People* (Colorado Springs: NavPress, 2019), 200.

Chapter Thirteen: A Way to Live Again

1. See Matthew 25:31–46.
2. William Willimon, *The Collected Sermons of William H. Willimon* (Louisville, KY: Westminster John Knox, 2010), 242.
3. John Irving, *A Prayer for Owen Meany* (New York: Ballantine, 1989), 278.
4. See Philip Yancey, *The Jesus I Never Knew* (Grand Rapids: Zondervan, 1995), 219–20.

Chapter Fourteen: Didymus

1. Genesis 3:19.
2. John 20:19.
3. See Luke 24:13–35.
4. See Luke 9:51–19:48.
5. Luke 9:51.
6. John 11:16.
7. Romans 12:2.
8. See Matthew 7:7–8; John 15:7; Matthew 21:22.
9. Thomas Merton, *Love and Living* (New York: Farrar, Straus and Giroux, 1979), 11–12.
10. Friedrich Nietzsche, *Human, All Too Human: A Book for Free Spirits* (Lincoln: University of Nebraska Press, 1996), 58.
11. Peter James Cameron, *Magnificat* 4, no. 12 (December 2001): 2–3; quoted in Christopher West, *Fill These Hearts: God, Sex, and the Universal Longing* (New York: Image, 2012), 7.

Chapter Fifteen: But Some Doubted

1. The New York City Housing Authority's low-income housing project, stretching from 14th Street to the South Street Seaport area along the East River, is the longest unbroken string of housing projects on the continent.

2. Dallas Willard, *Hearing God: Developing a Conversational Relationship with God* (1984; repr., Downers Grove, IL: InterVarsity, 1999), 218, emphasis in original.
3. Quoted in Viktor Frankl, *Man's Search for Meaning: An Introduction to Logotherapy* (Boston: Beacon, 1992), 152.
4. Pete Greig, *How to Pray: A Simple Guide for Normal People* (Colorado Springs: NavPress, 2019), 86.
5. David Brooks, "Making Modern Toughness," *New York Times*, August 30, 2016, www.nytimes.com/2016/08/30/opinion/making-modern-toughness.html.
6. "Malcolm Gladwell," Oprah's SuperSoul Conversations, season 9, episode 912, September 15, 2019, www.oprah.com/own-super-soul-sunday/malcolm-gladwell.
7. Elizabeth Kolbert, "Why Facts Don't Change Our Minds," *New Yorker*, February 20, 2017, www.newyorker.com/magazine/2017/02/27/why-facts-dont-change-our-minds.
8. Kolbert, "Why Facts Don't Change Our Minds."
9. Kolbert, "Why Facts Don't Change Our Minds."

Chapter Sixteen: My Lord and My God
1. Colum McCann, *Let the Great World Spin: A Novel* (New York: Random House, 2009), 325.
2. John 20:26 ESV, NASB, KJV.
3. Sue Monk Kidd, *When the Heart Waits: Spiritual Direction for Life's Sacred Questions* (New York: HarperOne, 2016), 22.
4. Anthony Bloom, *Beginning to Pray* (Mahwah, NJ: Paulist, 1970), 99.
5. John 20:16.
6. John 21:6, my paraphrase.
7. John 20:28.
8. Frederick Buechner, *The Faces of Jesus* (1974; repr., New York: Stearn/Harper & Row, 1989), 223.
9. *True Detective*, season 3 finale, created and written by Nic Pizzolatto, February 24, 2019, www.polygon.com/tv/2019/3/1/18244876/true-detective-season-3-finale-mystery-wayne-amelia-junius-watts.

10. Joseph W. Naus, *Straight Pepper Diet: A Memoir* (Brisbane, CA: KM Publishing, 2015), 34.
11. Søren Kierkegaard, *The Essential Kierkegaard*, ed. Howard V. Hong and Edna Hong (Princeton, NJ: Princeton University Press, 1978), 361.
12. John 19:30.
13. Dallas Willard, *Hearing God: Developing a Conversational Relationship with God* (1984; repr., Downers Grove, IL: InterVarsity, 1999), 132.
14. William H. Willimon, *Acts: A Bible Commentary for Teaching and Preaching* (Louisville, KY: Westminster John Knox, 2010), 51.
15. Gloria Steinem, "Anne Lamott Talks to Gloria Steinem about Writing, Kindness, and Making Sense of the Universe," *Cosmopolitan*, April 4, 2017, www.cosmopolitan.com/lifestyle /a9224345/anne-lammott-gloria-steinem-hallelujah-anyway.

Epilogue: Holy Saturday

1. These examples are adapted from John Ortberg, *Who Is This Man?* (Grand Rapids: Zondervan, 2012), 177.